# Turning the Tide
# of Battle

POCKET HISTORY

# Turning the Tide of Battle

Ingenious tactics
that secured
momentous victories

## Joseph Cummins

# CONTENTS

# Reinventing the Art of War

'**A**ccursed be he that first invented war.' Sixteenth-century English playwright Christopher Marlowe wrote these words in his play *Tamburlaine the Great*, demonstrating that, 500 years ago, as now, people understood that while fighting tooth-and-nail is probably innate to the human condition, war is not. War is a human invention—something to be imagined, concocted and refined.

*Turning the Tide of Battle* is a tour of the extraordinary ways in which innovative military commanders have invented and reinvented the art of war over the centuries. It is a history of unprecedented ideas from leaders who thought outside the box. Their unorthodox, often heretical, strategies changed the course of battles and, often, the course of history. Some became part of the military canon, most notably Hannibal Barca's carefully wrought trap at Cannae in Italy in 216 BC, which wiped out 50,000 Romans in a single day and has been emulated ever since. Others were desperate, one-off tactics devised on the spur of the moment, such as the decision by plague-ravaged Mongols besieging the town of Caffa on the Black Sea in 1347 to hurl their dead over the walls of the Christian enclave, thereby decimating its inhabitants.

A true tactician is not only concerned with deploying troops and weapons, but also with psychology. Thus, General Daniel Morgan, on the eve of the Battle of Cowpens during the War of American Independence, *knew* that his British opponent, Major Banastre Tarleton, a famously aggressive commander, would attack. Francisco Pizarro, leader of a group of conquistadors in 1530s South America, saw that the best way to get out of a situation in which he was surrounded by thousands of Inca troops was to snatch their ruler from right under their noses.

Courage, cunning, ingenuity, honed instincts and the ability to manufacture one's own luck—had all these traits been devoted to the more benevolent and enlightened aspects of the human condition, we might have had electricity, hip-hop and a cure for smallpox by, say, AD 1000. But instead we invented war. *C'est la guerre*—and good reading!

# CHAPTER ONE

## Whispers & Lies
### Themistocles & the Battle of Salamis, 480 BC

Early in the morning of 25 September 480 BC, 700 triremes—the battleship of choice in the ancient world—belonging to the Persian Empire lay in wait on one side of the narrow strait that separates the Greek mainland from the island of Salamis. To hear a roll call of the nationalities of the men on the Persian war vessels—Cicilians, Thracians, Lydians, Mysians, Bactrians, Phoenicians—is to hear, afresh, the sound of a lost and ancient world.

On a throne high on a hill above his fleet, with Athens, the city he had just set on fire, smoking behind him, stood Xerxes, the Great King of Persia, son of Darius, grandson of Cyrus the Great—'king', so his inscriptions read, 'of every country and every language, the king of the entire earth'. It was Xerxes' intention to spend the day watching his armada win a fabulous victory for his empire, an empire that stretched to modern Pakistan in the east, through central and western Asia to Macedonia in the north, and across the Sinai Peninsula to Egypt in the south.

Victory against the Greek fleet, which awaited him on the other side of the strait, near Salamis, seemed assured. After all, the Greeks possessed at most 370 triremes. More significantly, the evening before, his opponent, a blunt Greek general named Themistocles, had sent word to Xerxes via a slave that he was ready to betray his own countrymen and everything they stood for, and had advised Xerxes to attack immediately before the Greek forces fled.

What Xerxes didn't realise was that Themistocles' apparent betrayal was a ruse. Indeed, in one of the greatest deceptions of all time, Themistocles was gambling everything—his life, the lives of his family, the lives of his countrymen—on convincing Xerxes of his disloyalty, on the whisper of a slave into the ear of the King of Kings.

### Avenging Defeat at Marathon

As with the majority of wars, the Athens–Persia conflict of 480 BC had its origins in events that had occurred much earlier. Xerxes' father, Darius I, had extended the Persian Empire all the way into Macedonia, northeast of Greece. But in 490 BC, he had been defeated at the famous Battle of Marathon, on the Greek mainland, where a small force of Athenian infantrymen stopped his much larger army of Persians, forcing them to retreat back to Asia. Darius had died in 486 and his son Xerxes was hungry for revenge against the Greeks. He and his advisers planned their next campaign carefully. It was decided that the Persians would attack Athens both by land and by sea. They would come with over 1300 triremes and over 100,000 combatants, which included large forces of elite cavalrymen and crack infantrymen. In May of 480, Xerxes set forth to march to Greece, travelling north and west from Iran through Assyria, Thrace and Macedonia, and then into northern Greece.

One of the Greek soldiers at the Battle of Marathon—most likely a *strategos*, or commander— was an Athenian named Themistocles, who was known to be ill-educated and often ill-mannered (it is said that his father disowned him as a result), but also immensely crafty and ambitious. In 480, he was probably about forty-five years old and may have been the *archon*, or chief magistrate, of

Athens. At the very least, he was one of the city-state's most prominent military or political leaders. Unlike most of the Athenian leaders—and certainly unlike his opponent, the godlike Xerxes—he was not an aristocrat, but instead a blunt-spoken and pragmatic administrator.

Realising at least three years before the fact that the Persians were going to invade again, Themistocles had worked tirelessly to turn Athens into a first-class sea power, building a navy of over 200 triremes manned by 40,000 sailors. In the spring of 480, he convinced the Hellenic League—the confederation of Greek city-states that had organised to oppose Persia—that he should become the chief strategist in the defence of Greece.

In August, the Spartan commander Leonidas was sent with 8000 troops to defend the mountain pass at Thermopylae against the Persian land forces trying to enter from the north. For three days of brutal fighting, the Greeks, led by Leonidas' 300 Spartans, held off a force twenty times their size, before being betrayed by one of their own and slaughtered to the last man. Having achieved victory at Thermopylae, Xerxes and his army headed for the plains of Attica, and Athens.

Expecting this, Themistocles had already moved to evacuate the region and the city. All told, approximately 150,000 people lived in Attica at this time, including the city of Athens. In what was one of the greatest evacuations of its time, Themistocles sent the women and children to several different locations and ordered any man who could fight to make his way to the island of Salamis, which lies about 2 kilometres (1¼ miles) off the coast of Attica, just a short distance from Athens.

When Xerxes' soldiers entered Athens, they slaughtered the few citizens who had remained and set fire to the city. The Greeks waiting on Salamis could easily see the flames. They watched with horror and hatred in their hearts as their city steadily burned to the ground.

### An Extraordinary Gamble

By this time, twenty-two city-states of the Hellenic League had gathered forces on Salamis. Each had its opinion on how best to deal with the situation. Late on the night of 23 September and early into the next morning, fevered arguments raged. Many of the commanders wanted to flee to protect their homelands, or to stage a tactical retreat to the

Isthmus of Corinth, 40 kilometres (25 miles) away, where they could join up with Greek and Spartan infantry, who were preparing a last-ditch stand against the Persians. The arrival of the imposing Persian fleet, offering to do battle, on the afternoon of 24 September, lent weight to their arguments. When the Greek ships remained in their harbour, the Persians lingered almost tauntingly, and then slowly returned to their base at Phaleron, a small harbour to the southeast of Salamis.

Having learned through his extensive spy network that the Greeks on Salamis were squabbling among themselves, Xerxes sent columns of troops marching along the coast of Attica, heading to the Isthmus of Corinth. There were already plenty of Persian troops at Corinth, but Xerxes wanted the Greeks on Salamis to hear the thundering sound of, and see the dust rising from, their massed footsteps. The din went on into the night, and many Greeks began to panic. Some fled to their boats and had to be restrained from setting sail then and there. The situation on Salamis was spiralling out of control.

Only Themistocles, it seemed, realised that there was an opportunity here: a chance to fight a decisive battle. He knew that the large Persian naval force could not operate well in the confines of the Straits of Salamis, which were only 1.5 kilometres (1 mile) or so wide. The Persians' principal advantage—the ability to outflank their enemy using their numerical superiority—would be lost due to the narrowness of the waterway. The key to victory, he realised, was to incite Xerxes to do battle here—to make sure the Persian king committed his forces to this engagement and didn't choose one of the other options available to him, which included simply waiting the Greeks out until they starved or surrendered. But how could he achieve this?

Themistocles decided on an extraordinary gamble. Aware of the Persians' regular use of a spy network and intelligence from Greek traitors— one, Ephialtes, had helped secure victory for the Persians at Thermopylae by guiding them to a secret mountain pass from where they were able to outflank the Greeks—he decided to supply them with false intelligence, what would today be termed 'disinformation'. Not only that, he himself would supply this information, and send it directly to the Great King, Xerxes. And to make it all the more convincing, Themistocles would offer to be 'bought'.

The risks for Themistocles were enormous: he was literally staking everything on convincing Xerxes to attack. If Xerxes saw through his ruse, there were many things he might do—such as inform Themistocles' fellow Greeks that their commander was a traitor. There would have been no way for Themistocles to defend himself against this charge, since it was essential for him to keep his plan to himself. Had the Greeks thought him a traitor, he would have been executed and his family completely disenfranchised and dishonoured.

While his nervous commanders bickered, Themistocles sent his personal slave, Sicinnus, alone on a small boat, on a night-time mission to the Persian headquarters on the mainland. Sicinnus was a trusted retainer, the tutor of Themistocles' children, and he came from a small kingdom not far from Persia, so he might even have spoken some of that language. It is possible that Themistocles, expecting Sicinnus to be tortured, lied to his slave, making him believe that he really intended to defect. In any event, the slave was no doubt surrounded as soon as he came to shore— those first few minutes, with bristling Persian spears pointed at him, would have been perilous for

Sicinnus. But somehow he was able to convince the Persian soldiers that he carried with him a message for Xerxes from Themistocles, and he was taken to the Great King.

The Greeks were getting ready to flee, Sicinnus told Xerxes, and Themistocles was ready to go over to the Persian side. On behalf of Themistocles, he strongly urged Xerxes to mobilise his forces now, at night, to bottle the Greeks up in the Straits of Salamis. When the dawn came, Xerxes would then be able to pick off the disorganised and panicky Greek triremes one by one.

It must have been with a sigh of relief that Themistocles heard, later that night, a report that the dark shapes of Persian triremes had been observed moving out on both sides of the straits and across from the Greeks, blocking their exit. Now there was nothing for the Greeks to do but fight.

### The Battle for Greece

Shortly before 8 am on 25 September, as described by the Greek dramatist Aeschylus, who was present at Salamis, 'a song-like shout sounded triumphantly from the Greeks'. The waiting Persians heard it echo off the rocky confines of the strait. It was the paean, a huge cry uttered by thousands of Greek voices at once, both an invocation and a fearsome rebel yell. It told the Persians that the Greeks were not retreating this morning, but coming straight at them, ready to fight for their lives and liberty. For the crews of the Persian triremes, having rowed in place most of the night, this was not a welcome sound. Xerxes, watching high on his hill, could not have welcomed it either, but there was nothing he could do about it now. Themistocles had outwitted him, and the battle would now be joined.

The Battle of Salamis is one of those extra-ordinary moments that make lovers of history wish that they could enter a time machine and set the dial for 'Greece, 480 BC'. It would have been a spectacular scene, and the mind's eye fills to over-flowing with images.

Imagine 1000 brightly painted triremes, each with an eye of polished, painted marble on either side of the prow, being rowed furiously towards each other, three levels of oars striking the water, splashing up foam and spray. The Persian triremes, with their long, sleek rams, looked like swordfish; the Greek vessels, distinguished by their blunter, wider rams, were more like hammerhead sharks.

Imagine the rowers below decks, wearing only loincloths, sweating profusely, able to see nothing, hearing only the shouted directions of their rowing master and the piper keeping time on a shrill pipe. Imagine the helmsman of the ship, steering with double rudders, one in each hand, while the captain—normally the owner of the ship and the wealthiest man on board—shouted directions. The triremes would have constantly been closing up gaps in their ranks, much like a modern fleet of bombers on a mission, to make sure that no enemy would intrude to strike and ram.

Themistocles was out on the water behind his triremes, sitting on a large chair at the back of his vessel, directing through signal flags or possibly trumpets. Xerxes, on shore, had his aides call out to him the names of individual vessels, so that he could tell which were doing well and which were panicked and retreating.

As soon as the ships got within a few hundred metres of each other, the archers on board rained down arrows, and then each captain chose targets and attempted to break through the enemy ranks, either to ram or, in another crucial manoeuvre, to slash close to an enemy to break off his oars.

(Such an action would have required split-second coordination, since rowers on the attacking vessel were trained to pull in their oars just at the last moment, to keep them from snapping off.)

### The Greeks Prevail

As Themistocles had cleverly foreseen, as a result of the narrowness of the straits the Persians were unable to bring their superior numbers to bear— many Persian triremes were left waiting outside the straits, jockeying for their turn to enter. The Persians were also exhausted after having rowed for up to twelve hours. Furthermore, the Athenians fought with the ferocity of those fighting to preserve their homeland. Soon, the tide began to turn in favour of the Greeks.

After four or five hours, the Persians broke. Most of their triremes fled to the southeast, back to Phaleron. The Greeks began hunting out individual Persian triremes and ramming them mercilessly: 'They boned them like tuna or some catch of fish', wrote Aeschylus, his tone catching the bloodthirsty nature of the final hours of the battle. For days afterwards, Persian corpses covered the waters of the strait, and washed ashore both on Salamis and on the beaches of Attica. It is estimated that approximately 20,000 Persians lost their lives at Salamis. The Greeks sank perhaps 400 Persian ships and lost only 40 of their own.

After the battle, awards were given out to the bravest of the Greeks—those commanders whose ships had rammed and sunk the most Persian triremes, those warriors who had been the most daring in hand-to-hand combat. Themistocles was honoured, Herodotus writes, as 'the smartest man in all Greece'.

### Democracy is Born

On the day after the battle, Xerxes, who had lost a brother in the fighting, called a conference of all his commanders. He knew he had lost a great battle, but—since Persians did not measure themselves by ships at sea, but rather by the horses and men of their superb army—did not think he had lost the war. He ordered a general withdrawal, leaving behind his commander Mardonius with a portion of the army to keep a foothold on Greek territory until he could invade again. Mardonius camped out all winter, but, in the August of 479, he was killed and his army defeated by a united Greek army at

Plataea. At around the same time, the Greek navy attacked what was left of the Persian naval force, near the island of Samos, and destroyed it.

Although a few final battles remained to be fought against Persian domination, the Greeks were now free. Having achieved their great victory, they set about attempting to make an even greater peace. In 477, the Athenians founded and led the Delian League, an alliance of 150 Greek city-states. Under this league, the 'Golden Age' of Athens began, spawning dramatists such as Aeschylus, Aristophanes, Euripides and Sophocles, philosophers including Plato and Socrates, and historians like Thucydides and Herodotus.

Things did not turn out so well for Themistocles, however. The squabbling Athenians soon reverted to their distrust of this brave but not terribly political leader and he received no further honours. Worse was to come. In 464, the prime strategist of the Battle of Salamis found himself meeting the Great King of the Persians in a royal palace in Susa, not far from Persepolis. The Great King was not Xerxes, who had been assassinated in a palace intrigue two years before, but his son Artaxerxes. Themistocles had come, with his entire family, to work for his old enemy. Having been driven out of Athens by accusations that he took bribes and was a Persian agent (the former was probably true, but not the latter), he had landed here to spend his remaining years as governor of a Persian city.

# CHAPTER TWO

## Surround & Kill
Hannibal's double envelopment
at Cannae, 216 BC

The annals of the ancient world are filled with stirring tales of military leaders who achieved stunning success using unorthodox tactics: Cyrus the Great, Alexander the Great, Julius Caesar, to name but a few. But none of these heroes was a cooler battlefield strategist than a general named Hannibal Barca, from Carthage, in what is now Tunisia. (Barca, which meant 'lightning' in Punic, the language of Carthage, was not a surname but a description.) Hannibal's brilliantly unorthodox tactics resulted in many remarkable victories, but none greater than his triumph near the southern Italian town of Cannae, on a hot, dusty summer's day in 216 BC, which haunted the nightmares of Romans for generations and has influenced military thinking right up to the present day.

## The Punic Wars

During the course of two long wars in the third century BC, Carthage fought Rome for dominance over the Mediterranean. These wars were known as the Punic Wars, from the Latin word *Punicus*, meaning 'Phoenician', for Carthage had begun in the sixth or seventh century BC as a Phoenician mercantile colony, but eventually outstripped its origins. By the middle of the third century BC, it had become the pre-eminent power of the western Mediterranean, holding territory extending from southeastern Spain along the North African coast all the way to present-day Israel, including the islands of Corsica and Sardinia and the western half of Sicily. It was almost inevitable that Carthage would come into conflict with Rome, the great imperial power of the day, which by 264 BC, the date of the commencement of the First Punic War, had conquered most of the Italian Peninsula.

Sicily was the battleground of the First Punic War, which lasted twenty-three years—the longest conflict in ancient history. By 241 BC, the Romans had the upper hand; a peace treaty ensued, with Carthage handing over Sicily and being forced to pay an indemnity to cover Roman war costs. Trying to make up for what they had lost to Rome, the Carthaginians decided to expand their possessions in Spain. In the eyes of the Romans, Carthage posed a threat to Rome's western flank.

By 221 BC, Hannibal, the twenty-five-year-old son of a prominent Carthaginian commander, had become head of the Carthaginian armed forces. Hannibal besieged a Roman-sympathising city in Spain. When Rome protested and demanded that Carthage send Hannibal to Italy to face justice, the Carthaginian government replied by declaring war, and thus the Second Punic War began.

Little is known about Hannibal. No verifiable likenesses were left on coins or busts. His only intimates appear to have been his two brothers, Mago and Hasdrubal, who also served as his closest commanders. What we know for certain, however, is that Hannibal was devoted to Carthage and to the notion of defeating the Romans.

### Into the Lion's Den

As the Second Punic War began, Hannibal devised a plan that was both simple and daring. He would take his force of 30,000 infantry, 9000 cavalry and 40 war elephants over the Pyrenees, through the part of Gaul that is now southern France, and across the Alps into northern Italy—something that had never been done before.

Hannibal moved northwards from Spain during the summer of 218 BC. His was a polyglot army, including Carthaginians, Italians and Greeks, as well as more exotic soldiers—Numidian horsemen (Berbers from North Africa) who could ride without reins while they wielded both sword and spear; primitive Spanish clansmen who wore wolf and lion heads as helmets; Celtiberians from northern Spain and Portugal, who carried short, heavy spears with terrible piercing power.

Hannibal made his epic crossing of the Alps in fifteen days, losing some 12,000 men along the way and almost all his elephants. No one is quite sure which pass he took, but in November he appeared among the Gauls of northern Italy, a tribe only recently subjugated by the Romans. A Roman army led by Consul Publius Cornelius Scipio met Hannibal near the Ticino River, where their forces skirmished and Hannibal forced the Romans to withdraw. This was a small battle but a large victory for the Carthaginian commander, because it impressed the Gauls, who joined his command as allies when he promised them freedom and Roman spoils. Hannibal's forces swelled and he headed south, towards Rome.

On the face of it, Hannibal's journey through Italy was sheer madness. He was operating in enemy territory, with the only supplies available to him those he took from the land, and with an army that was minuscule compared to what the Romans could muster. Yet, in his year-and-a-half-long expedition down the length of the Italian Peninsula, Hannibal outwitted the Romans time and time again. At the Battle of the Trebbia River, which took place in northern Italy during late December 218 or early January 217 BC, Hannibal hid his forces in the misty half-light of early morning, on one side of the river, and lured the Romans into attacking by sending out his Numidian cavalry as bait. When the Romans charged across the river, Hannibal sprang his trap. Only 10,000 out of 40,000 Roman troops managed to fight their way out.

Hysteria mounted in Rome as Hannibal crossed the Apennines into central Italy. At some point during this arduous journey over rough country that included swamps and mountains almost as rugged as those of the Alps, Hannibal developed ophthalmia, an inflammation of the eye, which caused him to lose sight in one eye (although some sources claim this was a battle injury). Undeterred, the Carthaginian leader defeated another Roman army on the shores of Lake Trasimene (now Lake Trasimeno), early in May.

When news of this second disastrous battle reached Rome, the Senate decided to appoint a new commander in chief, the elderly but wise Quintus Fabius Maximus. He tried to shadow Hannibal without doing battle, to cut off his supply lines and deny his army vital sustenance, but Hannibal simply moved south through modern-day Apulia and Campania and directed his army to winter quarters on the Adriatic coast to rest his troops and replenish his supplies.

By 216, the Roman people had grown tired of Fabius' approach and had replaced him with two consuls, Lucius Aemilius Paullus and Gaius Terentius Varro, who were given command of a massive army numbering perhaps 80,000 men, although many of them were raw and inexperienced recruits. As this army was gathering, Hannibal and his forces moved about 100 kilometres (60 miles) south, to the small town of Cannae, which was uninhabited and half in ruins, but which contained important grain deposits. Then he prepared to wage the battle of his life.

## Arrayed for Battle

The exact site of the Battle of Cannae has not been definitively located, but was probably on a plain east of the present-day town of Monte di Canne, on the banks of the Ofanto River (the modern name for the ancient Aufidus River, which flowed east into the Adriatic Sea, about 5 kilometres [3 miles] away). The fight probably took place in early July—although some sources suggest August—when the heat would have been intense. Both the Romans and the Carthaginians made their camps on the north side of the river, but the ground was better on the south side, and Hannibal's forces arrayed themselves there, offering to do battle.

On the first day, the Romans did not accept this offer. But on the second morning they crossed the river and presented themselves on the plains of Cannae. More than twice the size of Hannibal's force, the Roman army was a fearsome sight, the world's most brutal fighting machine at that time. The Roman infantry were arrayed in maniples (meaning, literally, 'handfuls'), the basic tactical unit of the Roman army. There were thirty maniples per legion, each consisting of 120 men. The *hastati* were the first line of the infantry, the *triarii* the last, each composed of the most experienced soldiers. In between were the *principes*, usually the greenest soldiers, those who needed to be pushed forwards from behind and protected in front. Each heavy infantryman was equipped with his *gladius*, a short sword used mainly for stabbing; his *pilum*, the heavy Roman throwing spear; and his *scutum*, an oval shield, 1 metre (3 feet) long.

Hannibal, in fighting his way down the peninsula, had noticed that Roman legions operated best in phalanxes—large bodies of infantry, armed with spears and swords, which moved straight ahead in an armoured wedge in almost unstoppable fashion. He had also noticed that the commanders of these phalanxes were not trained to think independently: once the maniples moved forwards, they were committed to action and found it hard to adapt to changing circumstances.

The Roman right flank, almost flush against the river, consisted of cavalry led by Consul Paullus. Facing it, Hannibal placed his Spanish and Gallic heavy cavalry under the command of his brother Hasdrubal. On his far-right flank, facing more Roman cavalry, Hannibal positioned his brilliant Numidian cavalry under an aggressive and daring commander named Maharbal. The battle lines stretched across 4 kilometres (2½ miles).

In the centre of his line, Hannibal did something that was so at odds with conventional military wisdom that even the rawest lieutenant might have felt justified in looking askance at the Carthaginian leader. Instead of anchoring the centre of his front line with his most trusted heavy African infantry as usual, he replaced them with his lightly armed Gauls and Celtiberians, deliberately creating a weak centre. To make it all the more prominent, he bulged the front line forwards, so that it formed a crescent with its outer edge facing the enemy. On the left and right of this soft core he placed his most trustworthy infantry.

To the Romans, Hannibal's formation would have looked like a classic ancient battle array, which in fact matched their own: cavalry on the flanks, infantry in the centre. Playing into Hannibal's hands, Consul Varro, the overall Roman commander that day, decided to take advantage of his superior strength in numbers by massing his maniples in extra depth (rather than width) so that they could punch through Hannibal's central lines more easily. Unlike in other battles with Hannibal, there was no place on this battlefield where additional Carthaginian troops could be hidden to surprise the Romans, so Varro was sure the extra depth and force of his legions would carry the day.

## The Trap Closes

After both lines skirmished with light infantry, the two armies advanced on one another. As they did so, Hannibal extended his centre forwards even more, presenting an enticing target for the veteran Roman troops, who could sense weakness behind the bulge. In the meantime, cavalry from both sides met on the flanks in fierce fighting.

The centres of the armies then crashed together with a clash of arms and a clamour of war cries, the Romans throwing their spears from about 20 metres (65 feet), then attacking with their short swords, the Carthaginian forces replying with their own spears before swinging their curved, slashing swords. Dust swirled and the din was enormous as thousands of separate duels to the death took place.

Almost immediately, the Carthaginian lines began to give way as the lightly armed and armoured Gauls and Celtiberians fell back against the sheer physical weight of the Roman maniples—combat in the ancient world depended as much on weight and mass as individual fighting skill.

But then, on the Carthaginian army's left flank, Hasdrubal's cavalry routed the Romans and swung around behind the legions to attack the rear of the cavalry on the Romans' other flank, which was engaged in a fierce battle with Maharbal's Numidians. When Hasdrubal struck them from behind, they disintegrated.

By now, the Roman formation in the centre resembled a V, with its pointed tip pushing deeper and deeper into the Carthaginian lines. In the wild chaos of battle, the soldiers would not, immediately, have noticed that they were about to be surrounded. Hannibal, who was most likely positioned behind the centre of the Carthaginian lines along with his brother Mago, waited till just the right moment— then sprang his trap.

Probably using prearranged smoke signals, he sent the Carthaginian cavalry to attack the rear of the main Roman lines just as the heavy Carthaginian infantry came in from both flanks. The Romans were now completely encircled. The inexperienced troops of the second ranks, the *principes*, were hit with a shower of javelins from the side, which would have appeared suddenly, with horrifying effect, out of an almost impenetrable cloud of dust. The survivors turned to do battle, but were slaughtered by the far more experienced Carthaginians. The legionaries at the front of the battle, who had thought they were winning, now began to realise they were being attacked from all sides.

When the encirclement was accomplished, the slaughter began. It probably took most of the day. The Romans, crowded together, exhausted and terrified, possibly blinded by dust, were killed by the thousands. There were so many of them to be butchered that the Carthaginians took to slashing their hamstrings to cripple them, so they could be finished off the next day. Among the dead was the Roman consul Paullus. Consul Varro escaped, with perhaps 15,000 Roman troops, after they formed fighting wedges and slashed their way out.

By best estimates, 50,000 Romans lay dead on the field when the battle was over. This killing count for a one-day battle would remain unmatched until the first day of the Battle of the Somme in the First World War; and that, of course, was a battle fought over a huge front with modern weapons, including machine guns and artillery. Cannae remains one of the single bloodiest days of conflict in history.

## The Military Legacy

Hannibal was to wage war against Rome for another thirteen years. The Romans, having learned their lesson, avoided pitched battles as much as possible. Finally, in 202 BC, they managed to defeat Hannibal at the Battle of Zama in North Africa. The Carthaginian general went into exile, wandering the Mediterranean for some years. The Romans tracked him down on the shores of the Black Sea, in 182; the sixty-four-year-old general took poison rather than be brought back to Rome.

However, Hannibal's legacy, particularly the legacy of his innovative and unprecedented strategy at Cannae, has endured for centuries. As historian Will Durant has written, Cannae 'was a supreme example of generalship never bettered in history … and [it] set the lines of military tactics for 2000 years'. Indeed, it has proved an inspiration to generations of military thinkers, from Frederick the Great to US General Dwight Eisenhower. Most notably, Germany's Chief of Staff prior to the First World War, Count Alfred von Schlieffen, based his plan for an invasion of France and Belgium—an invasion that went ahead in 1914 (see p. 182)—on Hannibal's strategy at Cannae. American commander Norman Schwarzkopf also used a Cannae-style strategy during the First Gulf War, when in February of 1991 he enveloped the Iraqi army with two sweeping armoured wings from the south and west.

But almost no one has ever succeeded like the Carthaginian, Hannibal Barca.

# CHAPTER THREE

## Putting up Walls
### Caesar triumphs at Alesia, 52 BC

There has never been a military leader like Julius Caesar. Endlessly inventive and personally brave, he was apparently able to inspire loyalty in the most cynical and battle-weary legionary. And he seems to have enjoyed more than his fair share of good fortune. Indeed, so convinced of his luck was he that in one battle—wearing his distinctive *paludamentum*, or scarlet general's cloak—he stood out in front of his faltering army and allowed the enemy to rain iron spears down directly on him and him alone. Hundreds fell. Not one touched him.

Campaigning in Gaul from 58 to 52 BC, Caesar needed all the luck and skill he could muster, especially when he fought the last and most decisive battle of the war against a charismatic young leader commanding a tribe of fierce warriors in a supposedly impregnable hilltop fortress. Caesar's ambitions could have ended on the muddy earth of what is now south-central France, but, drawing on all his expertise (as well as his seemingly bottomless well of hubris), he managed to save the day for his legions and for himself.

But it was a near thing.

## A Ruthless Leader

After his assassination on the Ides of March in 44 BC, Caesar was officially declared a god, but his origins were somewhat more humble, if not without privilege. He was born in the year 100 BC (by means of Caesarean section, supposedly) to an aristocratic but relatively impoverished Roman family. After the premature death of his father, the sixteen-year-old Caesar became the head of his family. Caught up in a civil war raging at the time, he made some powerful enemies. He escaped into the army and spent two years campaigning in foreign countries, then returned to Rome and began building his reputation as a master politician and orator.

Yet he remained, first and foremost, a ruthless military man. During a journey to Rhodes in 75 BC, he was kidnapped by Sicilian pirates who held him for a ransom of fifty talents of gold. (They had intended to ask for twenty, but Caesar told them it was too little.) Caesar swore he would see them all crucified. They thought he was joking, but after he was ransomed, he returned, captured every one of them and hung them out to die on crosses.

In 63 BC, he became military governor of Iberia (Spain), where he quelled rebellious tribes. He returned to Rome in triumph to reign as co-consul along with the weak-willed Marcus Bibulus; the true ruling power of the country lay with what became known as the First Triumvirate, made up of Caesar and his political allies Pompey and Licinius Crassus. When, after five years, Caesar's term of office was over, he became governor of most of Gaul. He immediately set out in 58 BC to assert his authority over the territory.

## Among the Gauls

Gaul was, very roughly, modern-day France and Belgium, and, as Caesar famously wrote in his *Commentaries*—his own self-aggrandising account of his campaigns in Gaul—it was divided into three parts, consisting of the Belgae people (in the north), the Celts in central France, and the Aquitani to the south and west. Caesar marched into Gaul in 58 BC with the four veteran legions that had been given to him as governor, plus two others that he had raised in northern Italy. The Romans had already subjugated part of Gaul, particularly around the area of modern-day Provence, but the tribes to the north and west of the Rhône River were troublesome. Caesar may have decided to take them on because he wished to gain territory and the booty and glory of war, but it is also likely that he wanted to erase a hostile presence on Rome's northern borders—at an earlier time, about three centuries before Caesar's birth, Gauls had marched on Rome and sacked the city, and the citizens of Rome had never forgotten this.

Although the Gauls were members of different tribes, they shared certain characteristics. They were fierce warriors who practised animism, the worship of natural objects such as lakes, trees and mountains. They were physically striking, most having long, flowing hair (northern Gaul, where Caesar reckoned the tribes to be the wildest, because they were so far from the civilising influence of Rome, was sometimes called *Gallia Comata*, or 'long-haired Gaul'). There were about 300 tribes in all, totalling millions of people. The Romans were nearly always outnumbered, but usually managed to defeat their enemies by virtue of superior fighting tactics and clever politics—much of Caesar's campaigning involved turning certain tribes into Roman allies, while conquering others by force.

Caesar quashed the Belgae in the north and the tribes along the Atlantic seaboard in the west. He invaded Britain with two legions in 55 and 54 BC, invasions which some historians think were unnecessary, except to increase Caesar's prestige back home, which they certainly did. By then, all of Gaul appeared to be under control, though there was the occasional insurrection, as occurred in the winter of 54–53 BC, when Gauls in what is now Belgium nearly captured an entire garrison, until Caesar intervened. But such revolts were nothing compared to the one that would end the war—the one led by the great warrior Vercingetorix.

### Preaching Insurrection

Caesar wrote in his *Commentaries* that, by the winter of 53–52 BC, 'Gaul was now tranquillised'. But here Caesar was retrospectively justifying his departure, and this was not, in fact, the case. In the mountainous country of the Averni tribe, in south-central France—the modern Auvergne—a charismatic young nobleman named Vercingetorix was then fomenting rebellion.

Vercingetorix's father had been a powerful Gallic chieftain who had tried to become king of his tribe and had been murdered by rivals. Vercingetorix had apparently inherited some of his ambition. In January of 52 BC, the Carnute tribe near modern Orléans rose up and massacred Roman settlers who were coming to occupy the land. A wave of rebellion swept over France, and Vercingetorix, then probably in his early twenties, decided to ride it.

He began preaching rebellion against the Roman yoke, which scared the elders of his tribe so much that they ousted him from the Averni capital of Gergovia and its environs. From there, Vercingetorix wandered the region, fomenting insurrection. He appears to have been a compelling and magnetic figure, described as having curly reddish-blond hair and moustache, and being eloquent of speech. Going from village to village, he recruited so many to his cause that he was able to return to Gergovia and oust the elders who had ousted him. He now claimed the prize that had been denied his father: leadership of his people.

He ordered that arms be made—spears, swords and axes—and spent a good deal of time receiving the groups of warriors who arrived almost every day in response to his emissaries.

Next, Vercingetorix marched with thousands of men upon the tribes in the south of France who were loyal to Rome. The Romans had to react quickly. So Caesar raced from his winter quarters in northern Italy, picking up legions along the way, in order to cut off Vercingetorix and make him do battle.

## Scorched Earth

As Caesar pushed him back, Vercingetorix adopted a scorched-earth policy, burning all the settlements in the Romans' path, so that the countryside was filled with the smoking ruins of crops, farms, even entire towns. Vercingetorix retreated with his army to a camp outside Avaricum, the region's capital city (modern Bourges). He wanted to burn the city, but when those who lived in the region protested, he instead sent 10,000 men to help the city's 40,000 inhabitants hold out against Caesar.

Caesar's legions besieged Avaricum for twenty-five days, most of which were plagued by driving rains. Since the walls, made up in large part of great stones, were too tough to be knocked down by battering rams, the Romans tried to break the stones off one by one using huge hooks attached to long poles. The Gauls, in reply, lassoed the hooks with long ropes and winched them over the walls by means of windlasses. When the Romans tried to tunnel under the walls, the Gauls replied by digging their own tunnels to undermine the Roman ones. But eventually, the Romans were able to build a huge siege-tower, push it against the wall and climb into the city. Furious at having been stymied for so long, the legionaries slaughtered, according to Caesar's count, 40,000 men, women and children, while only 800 managed to escape to join Vercingetorix.

The armies of Vercingetorix and Caesar then raced each other to the Averni capital of Gergovia; Vercingetorix won by a nose, quickly fortified the city and was able to repulse the Romans and inflict heavy losses—Caesar's first defeat in battle. Vercingetorix's victorious troops chased after the retreating legions and were only stopped by the legendary Legio X, which Caesar rallied personally to stand in the way of the advancing Averni. Even so, as the Gauls withdrew to Gergovia, they could still savour a great victory. They had in their possession several of the sacred standards of the legions and had, according to some historians, wiped out at least 6000 Roman troops.

Caesar left the area of Gergovia and marched south, while Gallic tribes flocked to Vercingetorix's side. Feeling powerful, the Averni leader attacked Caesar's cavalry with his own but was badly beaten during a pitched battle near modern-day Dijon, in part because the Roman army had been reinforced with German mercenaries from across the Rhine. Vercingetorix's troops were sent reeling back, and Caesar, sensing the advantage, followed up quickly with his 60,000 troops.

Unwilling—wisely—to meet Caesar on an open field of battle, where the trained fighting power of the legions would more than make up for the fact that the Gauls outnumbered them, Vercingetorix then took his 80,000-strong army to the town of Alesia, about 50 kilometres (30 miles) from modern Dijon. There, he would make his stand.

### A Field of Horrors

Situated atop Mont Auxois, Alesia was a fortified town, bulwarked by deep trenches and heavy, stone walls. To assault it would have been suicidal, and

Vercingetorix thought, rightly, that Caesar did not have enough men to invest it effectively. It was now September of 52 BC. If Vercingetorix could hang on for a few months, Caesar would have to retreat to a winter camp and Vercingetorix would be seen by all his people as the victor. But the Averni leader, as brave and charismatic as he was, had not counted on Caesar's perseverance and ingenuity.

Caesar immediately set to work building one of the most extraordinary siegeworks that has ever been built, a wall that ran all the way around Alesia. It was the kind of construction known in military terminology as a circumvallation, and it was designed to make sure the Gauls were blockaded inside their fort and to protect the besieging Romans from raiding parties from Alesia.

Caesar's palisade was about 4 metres (13 feet) high, roughly 16 kilometres (10 miles) in circumference, and had twenty-three small forts dotted along its perimeter. The walls were made of thick tree trunks from trees obtained from nearby forests. Sharpened branches—'like stag's horns', as Caesar recorded in his *Commentaries*—were affixed to the outer walls every metre or so to impale anyone trying to climb up them.

Between the city walls and the palisade, for about 400 metres (1300 feet) directly in front of their lines, the Romans created a field of horrors. Nearest Alesia, they placed rows of *stimuli*, wooden blocks fixed with iron spikes 30 centimetres (12 inches) long. Outside these were fields of ironically named 'lilies'—sharpened stakes in pits. Closest to the palisade were two deep parallel trenches, one filled with diverted streamwater, the other empty.

Vercingetorix, looking out from his battlements, would have realised that the Romans were here to stay and known, too, that his men had only thirty days' worth of rations. He ordered his cavalry to attack the Romans and try to halt their construction work, but the German mercenaries once again routed the Gauls. As, after three weeks, the Roman fortification neared completion, Vercingetorix sent more of his cavalry out under the cover of darkness to try to break through; though most were killed, a few managed to escape the German mercenaries.

## Walling Themselves In

Caesar found out by interrogating captured Gauls that these escapees had asked other tribes to assist Vercingetorix. Caesar was aware that if the Gauls attacked in number from the rear, the Romans could be obliterated. Despite having little time to analyse the situation fully, he came up with what one historian has called 'one of the most brilliant siege tactics in the history of warfare'.

Caesar had a second wall built behind the first, facing outwards, in the direction from which the relief forces might come. This second wall, known as a contravallation and also made of wood, entirely encircled the first wall; its wider circumference made it 25 kilometres (16 miles) round. Between the two walls, there was room for the entire Roman army. After completing the second wall in a few weeks, Caesar waited. In the meantime, conditions inside Alesia were terrible, with many thousands of women and children starving alongside their warriors. When the Gauls sent them outside the walls of Alesia, hoping the Romans might let them through, to food and safety, Caesar, unable to risk opening his wall, left them where they were, to starve.

## Attacked from Both Sides

In late September, reinforcements came thundering up the valley to aid the Gauls. Caesar wrote that about 250,000 barbarians arrived to support

Vercingetorix, but most historians estimate the number at around 100,000. This relief force at once attacked the outer Roman wall, while Vercingetorix launched an attack from within Alesia on the inner wall. The hard-pressed Roman legions were forced to fight on two fronts, but at least had protection on both sides. Had Caesar not erected the second palisade, it is almost certain that the legions would have been massacred. The battle raged all day with Caesar, sporting his red *paludamentum*, seemingly everywhere, on both ramparts. By sunset, neither side had gained the advantage.

The next day, 2 October, the final attack of the Battle of Alesia was launched. The Averni had discovered a weakness in the Roman walls—a place where, because of the irregular shape of the slopes of Mont Rea, the mountain that abutted Mont Auxois near Caesar's defences, the palisades did not quite meet. The relief force and Vercingetorix's forces had managed to communicate well enough to launch a coordinated attack against this place and, in desperate fighting, the Romans were nearly overwhelmed, in some places being outnumbered six to one. Vercingetorix's Gauls came prepared: they filled the trenches with dirt, and, locking their shields over their heads, made it to the ramparts, where they hurled grappling hooks over the palisades and tried to pull them down. The Romans threw iron spears down on them from above.

Every soldier, both Roman and Gaul, knew that this battle was the one that counted—there would be no quarter given. The relief forces attacking down the slopes of Mont Rea had great momentum and came crashing against the outer walls, shaking them to their foundations, while Gauls who had come down the slopes from Alesia, on the other side of the Roman enclosure, hurled spears into the palisades, killing hundreds of Romans.

Then, when the battle seemed most desperate, Caesar did what Caesar always seemed to do: threw himself in harm's way and saved the day. Sensing weakness in one flank of the Gallic relief force, Caesar personally led Roman cavalry and infantry outside the ramparts to flank the Gauls. The surprised enemy was routed, with thousands killed and captured, and Vercingetorix retreated to his fortress, knowing he had to surrender.

The following morning, in a celebrated scene, Vercingetorix rode a dashing charger in a full circle around where Caesar and his officers sat. Then, leaping down, he hurled his sword and spear to the ground—and then sat in front of Caesar in submission. The surviving Averni were given to Caesar's triumphant legions as slaves—each Roman soldier received one Gaul.

## The End of Gaul

Vercingetorix became Caesar's prisoner and was taken to Rome in chains and imprisoned for six years. Then, after Caesar was named emperor in 46 BC, Vercingetorix—by then a wasted wreck of his former self, although probably no more than thirty years old—was paraded before the Roman people before being garrotted.

The war in Gaul was more or less over, although the Gauls would rise in rebellion from time to time. But ultimately, they became staunch Roman allies until the fall of the Roman Empire in AD 476. All thanks to Caesar's quick thinking and the double row of palisades he built across a muddy hilltop.

# CHAPTER FOUR

# 'God Belonging'
## Mongol suicide squads at the Battle of Liegnitz, 1241

On a spring day in 1241, Duke Henry II of Silesia, also known as Henry the Silent, passed through his home city of Liegnitz at the head of a long procession of soldiers. He was on his way to do battle with a terrifying threat not only to Poland but also to all of Europe: the 'Tartar' hordes who had poured in from the east, seeking plunder and blood. They had already defeated—destroyed may be a better word—two armies. Duke Henry's force was the last in Poland that stood in their way.

Large crowds watched the duke's progression, praying. But as he passed by the venerable church of St Mary's, a stone fell off the roof, nearly striking and killing him. He proceeded, but both he and the bystanders saw this as an evil omen. As it turned out to be. By the end of that day, Henry would be dead and his army obliterated following an astonishing display of Mongol ferocity and battle tactics such as these Christian knights had never seen before.

The Battle of Liegnitz was a clash, not just between two armies, but between two continents and two utterly alien cultures. The knights believed in the complete superiority of their civilisation and their Christian faith, to the exclusion of all other cultures and religions; they considered most races aside from Europeans to be inferior, if not subhuman. On the other hand, and perhaps surprisingly, the Mongols, although they could be stone-cold killers, allowed religions in conquered countries to flourish and even adopted customs of foreign peoples as their own, when this proved useful.

This flexibility was also the key difference when it came to strategy. Generally, the proud Christian knights, usually wearing full armour and waving banners and standards, knew only how to charge straight ahead and kill. In contrast, the Mongols had learned from their long campaigns over varied territories how to adapt to every new situation. When the lightly armed Mongol troops charged, it was always with a specific purpose. And at Leignitz that purpose was to deceive.

## The Stuff of Nightmares

There are some historians who believe that the Mongol invasion of Europe in the winter and spring of 1241 haunted an entire continent for centuries to come. It wasn't just the immediate physical scars— the thousands who died or were wounded in battle, and the thousands of others who died of starvation from the ensuing famines in a huge swath of land from the Baltic Sea to the Danube—but the psychological ones. 'Against the wrath of the Tartars, O Lord, deliver us' was a prayer used well into the twentieth century by churches in parts of Hungary, Poland and Russia. After 1241, there was a widely held and enduring fear that Europe was constantly vulnerable—open to terrifying, inexplicable and savage attack from the east.

'Tartars' was just one of the many names the Europeans gave the Mongol forces under the dual command of the late Genghis Khan's grandson, Batu, and the illustrious Mongol general Subotai. The word 'Tartar' comes from the Latin *Tartarus*, meaning 'hell', which the European clergy felt these horsemen had sprung from. Some commentators attached 'dog-faced' as an adjective when describing the invaders, as in 'dog-faced Tartars', possibly because the hats of rank-and-file Mongol soldiers were made of dog skin. In Germany, it was said that the Mongols were a lost tribe of Israel, their invasion secretly aided by European Jews, which led to numerous travelling Jewish merchants being murdered. It was also said that the Tartar soldiers ate the bodies of the dead and especially enjoyed feasting on breasts ripped from young women. The reality was, of course, somewhat different, though the Europeans had good reason to be afraid.

Before Genghis Khan was born in 1162 (his real name was Temujin; Genghis Khan means 'Great Lord'), the nomads on the steppes of eastern Asia lived a feudal existence, each tribe led by its khan and divided into patriarchal clans. The ambitious and energetic Temujin changed all this. By 1206, with a loyal band of followers, he had conquered and united the tribes of central Asia, and acquired the name by which he has since been known. He went on to triumph over China, Afghanistan and Persia, after which his forces (led by his two generals, or *orloks*, Subotai and Jebe) attacked Georgia in 1221—giving Christian Europe a foretaste of Mongol violence—and swept back through Russia, winning every battle they fought.

## Lust for Conquest

Europe was spared for the next twenty years; Genghis Khan died in 1227 and the Mongols, under his son Ögödei, were kept busy consolidating their gains in Asia. The society they set up in conquered territories was, in some ways, a fair one. They permitted subjugated communities freedom of worship, and instituted improved legal, postal and transportation systems. At the same time, the Mongols remained essentially a warrior people, whose main *raison d'être* was conquest—and not so much, it seemed, for the sake of plunder and territory as for the sheer exhilaration of combat.

The Mongol army was, without question, the best fighting force of the thirteenth century. Any man over twenty in the Mongol Empire, with a few highly specific exceptions (such as those whose profession was to wash the bodies of the dead), had to be in the army. Divided into organisational units of multiples of ten, from the *arban* (ten men) to the *touman* (10,000 men), the army was highly trained and extremely loyal. Mongol forces were made up almost entirely of cavalry and Mongols were the best riders in the world, able to stay on their horses literally all day, if necessary, eating yogurt and dried meat that they stored in their saddlebags. In combat, these men were ferocious, shooting arrows from small but powerful bows. They gave no quarter and asked for none, killing pitilessly and remorselessly, often tracking their enemies over great distances, like wolves.

And they looked the part: beneath their hats of dog and monkey skin, the older soldiers in particular, their faces a welter of scars from the gashes they inflicted on themselves to keep their beards from growing, were terrifying to their enemies.

## Feigning Retreat

It wasn't just the ferocity of the soldiers that set the Mongols apart, however; it was also their battlefield tactics. One of the most innovative and effective tactics they developed was to pretend to retreat in the face of an approaching enemy—to turn around and run, in other words—and, when the enemy gave chase, to lead them deeper and deeper into a trap, where the main Mongol forces would leap from cover and annihilate them.

This was far from an easy job. For one thing, turning your back to an advancing foe is a good way to get ridden down and killed, despite the fact that Mongols were known for their ability to twist around in their saddles and shoot arrows behind them with great accuracy. For another, in order to tempt opponents into chasing you, you have to be few in number (so that they are not too intimidated) and also get very close to their lines (so that you are a tempting target).

This dangerous job was given to the Mongol light infantry, who were called the *mangudai*. The word literally means 'God belonging', and could be rendered as 'already with God'. That is, 'already dead'—a convenient way to think of yourself when acting as mouse before a very large and nasty cat. *Mangudai* were volunteers; in fact, in a society with such a fierce warrior ethic, this chance to prove your bravery was highly coveted. (Some historians believe that these men came only from two specific Mongol tribes, the Uru'ut and Maghut, who were known for their utter fearlessness.) Essentially, the *mangudai* were suicide troops.

When an enemy force had been located, the *mangudai*, armed only with bows and arrows and light shields, would ride ahead of the main Mongol army and attack their foe recklessly. When their opponents saw how few they were, they almost always attacked in force, at which point the Mongol horsemen would gallop back the way they had come, enticing the enemy to follow them, further and further and further—until the main Mongol forces sprung their trap. Developed and refined through decades of conflict in Asia, the strategy would be used to devastating and terrifying effect at the Battle of Leignitz.

## The Mongol Invasion of Europe

It is common for conquerors to seek a pretext for actions that are essentially founded on greed. The Mongols were no exception. Having consolidated their eastern territories, they turned with hunger to the west. Their excuse for attacking Europe was that King Béla IV of Hungary was harbouring their sworn enemies, the Cumans, a nomadic people the Mongols had driven out of the steppes.

Batu wrote a note to Béla in December of 1240, which, almost eight centuries later, is notable for its blunt cruelty:

> *Word has come to me that you have taken the Cumans, our servants, under your protection. Cease harbouring them or you will make me*

*an enemy because of them. They who have no*
*houses and dwell in tents will find it easy to*
*escape. But you who dwell in houses within*
*towns—how can you escape me?*

Béla rejected this ultimatum, and the Mongols prepared for war. The attack on Europe was planned
and led by Subotai, the great Mongol general.
While his main force of perhaps 120,000 men
headed for King Béla and Hungary, he sent a much
smaller force, perhaps 20,000 strong, north into
Poland under the command of Ögödei's son Kadan
and nephew Baidar. This army was essentially a
diversionary force; Subotai hoped that the presence
of Baidar and Kadan in Silesia and Poland would
keep the armies there occupied and render them
unable to help in the defence of Hungary.

February 1241 saw harsh winter weather, the
kind of conditions in which no European army
would generally campaign. But to the Mongols
the weather was almost meaningless. Baidar and
Kadan burned the cities of Lublin and Zawichost
and numerous small villages in-between, killing
men, women and children alike, and stealing any
livestock or stored grain they could get their hands

on. The Vistula River froze and the Mongols crossed it to burn the town of Sandomierz. Yet, no army came out to meet them.

Since their goal was not conquest but to draw forces away from Hungary, Baidar and Kadan split their army and swept through Poland and Bohemia, laying waste to these regions. Then word came that Henry the Silent had assembled an army, so Baidar and Kadan rejoined their forces and marched hurriedly to Liegnitz, the present-day Polish city of Legnica, to meet him.

### Setting the Trap at Liegnitz

Going into the Battle of Liegnitz, the forces assembled under the banner of Henry the Silent totalled approximately 25,000 men, slightly more than faced them on the Mongol side. But although Henry's own army was made up of trained knights and his forces included contingents of Knights Templar and Teutonic Knights, who were superb fighters, the majority of his men were poorly trained conscripts and volunteers, mainly peasants and gold-miners. The Mongol fighters, veterans of long-lasting and wide-ranging Asian campaigns, possessed far more combat experience.

The two forces met on a plain now known as Walstadt ('the chosen place'), not far from Liegnitz. Henry carefully arrayed his forces: his Silesian knights and the Knights Templar and Teutonic Knights in the centre of his lines, his less experienced peasants and miners on the outer edges. Henry did not know that King Wenceslaus was only a day's march away with an army of about 50,000 men, or he might not have chosen to do battle. In contrast, Baidar and Kadan, as a result of their superior intelligence system, were aware of the approach of Wenceslaus. Therefore, they decided to do battle immediately.

Baidar and Kadan sent out a skirmishing force of *mangudai*, which rode straight across Henry's front, shooting arrows with deadly accuracy from a range of less than 100 metres (330 feet). There were at most several hundred of them. Henry saw that the force was small, and committed knights and the Teutonic fighters to the battle. The *mangudai* took heavy losses and retreated, but then wheeled, stood their ground and began firing arrows again.

Now Henry made a fatal mistake: he charged with everything he had—all his cavalry, the Knights Templar and Teutonic Knights, and his Silesian knights. The *mangudai* broke and ran to the rear, and the Christian knights, praising heaven for their good fortune, chased them ferociously.

This pursuit is what the typical knight of the Middle Ages lived for—heavily armoured on his stout and valiant warhorse, chasing down a more lightly armed enemy, prepared to hack him to pieces with axe or broadsword in the name of Christ and country. As the Christian forces gained speed, their momentum became almost unstoppable. The Mongol horsemen remained, tantalisingly, just beyond their reach, occasionally turning and firing arrows, but for the most part seeming to run on in panic, their pony's eyes rolling. Certain that a magnificent victory would be theirs, the knights bore down harder, waving their swords, preparing to come in for the kill.

### Routed & Slaughtered

Then the trap was sprung. Mongol archers who had been hidden on the flanks suddenly appeared and shot arrows into the knights from the side. Other Mongol warriors let off smoke bombs to the rear of Henry's knights—the use of smoke and explosives was something the Mongols had picked up from the Chinese—cutting them off from the rest of their army. Reeling in shock and surprise, the knights reined in their horses, but were quickly surrounded by five or ten warriors at a time, who shot arrows into the Christian steeds, causing them to collapse to the ground.

The Mongol heavy cavalry then rode in for the kill, wielding their sharp lances and curved swords, wreaking havoc among the confused knights, who only a few moments before had thought that they were winning the battle. Fighting on foot, with their horses dead around them, the knights were easily run down. The Knights Templar fought bravely but were killed to the last man, as were the Teutonic Knights and 500 others.

In the meantime, Henry's infantry were easily routed and slaughtered. Henry tried to flee but was chased down by determined Mongol riders, who killed him, cut off his head and mounted it on a spear. This horrible trophy they paraded outside the walls of Liegnitz, where most of the citizens of the region were now cowering. They then cut off the right ears of the Christian dead to send to Batu, as evidence of their great victory. It was said that they filled nine bags full.

## Turning Defeat into Victory

As the army of King Wenceslaus neared, Baidar and Kadan realised that they didn't have enough strength to face him in a head-on battle. Therefore, they decided to keep Wenceslaus pinned down in Poland for a while; they feinted to the west, drawing him in that direction. Then, when he committed his forces, the Mongols broke up into small groups and headed south towards Hungary, burning and pillaging as they went.

In the meantime, on 11 April, Subotai's main army engaged King Béla's Hungarians at the Battle of Mohi and utterly destroyed them. Soon, the Mongols closed in on Vienna, getting near enough to view its church spires. They also forged south—a reconnaissance force appeared just 100 kilometres (60 miles) or so north of Venice, striking terror into the hearts of the Italians.

But then the Tartars disappeared. While all of Europe prayed, this mysterious foe turned around and left. The religious thought that God had answered their supplications. Perhaps he had. The Mongols, however, were returning to central Asia for a very specific reason: Ögödei had died and a new khan needed to be elected. Europe, which had lain open for the taking, was saved, but permanently affected. Large areas of Poland were so depopulated by the Mongols that they had to be resettled with German immigrants.

The average Polish person at the time did not know who the Mongols were, or why they had attacked Poland and destroyed its finest knights at Liegnitz. The smoke screen used in the battle by the Mongols, and possibly also the strong incense they often burned around their camps, gave rise to a myth that Henry's forces had been killed, not in fair combat, but by a mysterious gas attack.

The Polish people began to believe that Henry's sacrifice at Liegnitz was in fact a Pyrrhic victory, one that heroically delayed the Mongols. Indeed, for centuries afterwards, the families of certain nobles who had participated in the battle wore the Mongol cap as a sign of honour.

In retrospective accounts of the Battle of Liegnitz, the number of Mongols arrayed on the field was frequently inflated, sometimes as much as fivefold. This was probably because the Mongols' ingenious tactics made it *seem* like they were everywhere at once. In fact, the Polish forces had simply been completely outmanoeuvred and utterly destroyed by the Mongols' superior military expertise and, in particular, by the fearlessness and cunning of the *mangudai*, who had ridden out and enticed the Christian knights into a foolish and ultimately catastrophic battle.

# CHAPTER FIVE

# Death in the Air
## The siege of Caffa, 1347

One day in the spring of 1347, a Mongol khan on the shores of the Black Sea made a desperate decision. For months, he had been watching his men die around him from a terrible disease which raised egg-like swellings in the armpits and groin, bruised the skin in spots until it was purple and black, brought on horrible, quivering fevers and caused men to shriek hysterically as they died, reeking of vomit and excrement. Yet, if Janibeg—for that was the khan's name—looked to the shining walls of the city his army was besieging, he could see his enemies, apparently unaffected, laughing at his weakening and dying warriors, and thanking God that they had been spared this pestilence.

The Mongol army was becoming feeble—at least half of its 40,000 men had died. It no longer had a hope of defeating the Christians holed up in their whitewashed port city. But, in true Mongol fashion, Janibeg decreed that his antagonists would not escape unscathed—that the curse that God had visited upon his people would also be felt inside the city.

Commanding those men who could still function, he set them to their catapults and trebuchets. However, instead of having them mount rocks or containers of naphtha, ready to be lit, in the slings, he had them load up the gruesome corpses of their deceased comrades-in-arms, men who had died of this mysterious plague before they were able to inflict a blow on the enemy. At least in death, they might do some good.

Janibeg raised his arm. When he brought it down, the reeking, rotting corpses flew tumbling and turning through the air, like twisting, life-size puppets, into the town of Caffa, where they landed with a splatter and a spray of blood.

And so began one of the most extraordinary episodes of biological warfare on record.

### Flourishing through Trade

In the mid thirteenth century, Caffa (now Feodosiya in the Ukraine) was a sleepy fishing village on the north shore of the Black Sea, which had the misfortune to occupy a strategic location at a time when the West and the East were vying for control of the region. Caffa was part of the great Mongol Empire, begun by Genghis Khan in 1206, which had spread across China, the steppes of Russia, central Asia and Asia Minor, and right to the edge of Europe. Much of Europe had been horrified by the Mongol threat—these so-called Tartar hordes had retreated in 1241 only because the great khan Ögödei, son of Genghis himself, had died (see p. 65)—but not the intrepid merchants of the Italian city-state of Genoa. From the very beginning, these men had seen the incursions of the Mongols as an opportunity for unprecedented trade.

Located on the northwest coast of Italy, Genoa was a small but powerful city-state, one of the peninsula's maritime republics, and the Genoese were known as brilliant seafarers and crafty merchants. By the 1250s, they had made trading agreements with the burgeoning Mongol Empire and in 1266 they leased the village of Caffa from the Tartars and set about making it a major trading centre.

Caffa was perfectly situated to receive goods from all points of the compass: timber and furs from the north; silk and spices and diamonds from

Indonesia; silver, gold and cotton from the west; and slaves from all over, for under the Genoese Caffa became one of the biggest slave markets in Europe, a place where Mongols, Muslims and Christians could both unload and purchase human flesh. Within eighty years, the population of Caffa had grown to about 70,000, and the settlement had become one of the most influential port cities in the known world.

### 'Dreadful Signs and Portents'

The early fourteenth century was a time of terrible portent in Europe. The so-called Little Ice Age had begun, bringing frigid weather and massive blizzards that lasted well into the spring and destroyed crops. In about 1315, a terrible famine hit northern Europe, and humans as well as livestock died, and those who did not die were severely weakened by malnutrition. As if that wasn't enough, reports of strange and disturbing events came out of the East. Gabriel de' Mussis, the Italian scribe and notary who would later record the horrors of Caffa for history, wrote: 'In the Orient at Cathay … where the world's head is … dreadful signs and portents have appeared'. Supposedly, there were immense swarms of locusts, torrential rains followed by blistering droughts, earthquakes that swallowed cities and mountains whole, and entire provinces assailed by poisonous snakes and scorpions. In fact, while some of these reports were fantasy and exaggeration, there was massive upheaval in China at this time. The country had been involved in a lengthy rebellion against the Mongol conquerors, which caused widespread suffering and death, with large swaths of land laid utterly to waste.

Even more ominously, a strange pestilence had arisen, one that seemed to emerge out of nowhere to wipe out an entire village before reappearing in the next village with the same mortal force. Historians now know that this was the bubonic plague, the so-called Black Death, which was soon to kill one in every two people in China and one out of every three people in Europe, central Asia, India and the Middle East. (If the Black Death hit the world today with the same ferocity, and we had no defences against it, it would claim approximately 2 billion lives.) The Black Death was carried by the bacillus *Yersinia pestis*, which preyed on rats and other rodents (although this was not known until the twentieth century), and also spread by human contact with the bacteria. When environmental upheavals, such as floods, famines, war and earth-quakes, hit, wild rats leave forests in search of food, which almost inevitably takes them to human communities. In early-fourteenth-century China, that meant communities where immune systems had been considerably weakened by starvation and stress, and where hygiene and sanitation (never good to begin with) were nonexistent. These were perfect conditions for *Yersinia pestis* to begin its journey through the human population, and the trade routes along the broad steppes of Mongolia and central Asia were the perfect highway.

In 1334, plague struck the Chinese province of Hubei; by 1339, it had reached Lake Issyk Kul, in northwestern China, a stopping point for travellers. The next centre where merchants met was Caffa, 1600 kilometres (1000 miles) to the southwest.

### Beginning with a Brawl

It's ironic that one of history's most significant instances of large-scale biological warfare began with what was essentially a street fight. In 1343, Genoese from Caffa were trading in the town of Tana, on the Don River, just up the river from the

Sea of Azov, which flows into the Black Sea. The local Muslims and Mongols traded with the Genoese, but didn't particularly like them. They thought them vain and egotistical, and crooked in their business dealings. For their part, the Genoese were suspicious of the foreign ways of the Easterners. According to Gabriel de' Mussis, who was not there but heard the story from those who were, a Muslim merchant in Tana thought a Genoese was cheating him. Words were exchanged, a fight ensued and a Genoese pulled a knife and killed the merchant.

The Muslim community then appealed to the Mongol khan, Janibeg, a Muslim himself and their protector, for help. Janibeg, always ready to beard a Christian or two, showed up with a large Tartar force and attacked. The outnumbered Genoese retreated to their boats, and set sail west for Caffa. They could see the Mongols riding their horses along the shoreline, trying to beat them there. The Genoese made it first, raised the alarm and closed the gates of their city. De' Mussis described it this way: 'See how the heathen Tartar races, pouring together from all sides, suddenly invest Caffa … The trapped Christians … hemmed in by an immense army, could hardly breathe'.

There then ensued a seesaw battle that was to last, on and off, for four years. The Mongols tried to starve the Christians out, but the Genoese had sufficient provisions and water to stay put almost indefinitely. In February 1344, the siege was temporarily lifted when a Genoese relief force arrived and defeated Janibeg's forces decisively, killing approximately 15,000 Mongols.

Janibeg, however, was not about to allow the Christians to escape unscathed. He came back in 1345, this time with a larger force and many more siege machines, ready to invest Caffa, destroy its walls and butcher all of its inhabitants. But, then, as de' Mussis recorded:

> *Behold, the whole army was infected by a disease which overran the Tartars and killed thousands upon thousands every day. It was as though arrows were raining down from heaven to strike and crush the Tartars' arrogance. All medical advice and attention was useless; the Tartars died as soon as the signs of disease appeared on their bodies: swellings in the armpits or groin caused by coagulating humours, followed by a putrid fever.*

This was obviously a Christian point of view—God was smiting the heathens—but it is understandable that the Genoese in Caffa might have felt grim pleasure in seeing the suffering of their tormentors. During the four-year siege, trade had nearly come to a standstill and thousands had died.

The accursed Mongols were feeling the wrath of Almighty God. It wouldn't be long now, the Genoese thought, before these Eastern fiends would have to turn tail and drag themselves back up the Don to where they came from—those who hadn't already been sent to *Tartarus*, that is, to Hell.

### A Hard Rain

People in medieval times had no real idea of the nature of infectious disease, but those who came in contact with this deadly plague certainly knew that it was transmitted from person to person, in some fashion. It may be that Janibeg knew this, and that it led him to implement his fiendish and devastating ploy. Of course, using the bodies as projectiles not only helped assuage Janibeg's thirst for revenge, but also solved his body-disposal problem. Whatever his reasons, Janibeg's strategy had a devastating effect, as de' Mussis recorded:

*[The Tartars], fatigued by such a plague and pestiferous disease, stupefied and amazed, observing themselves dying without hope of health, ordered cadavers placed on their hurling machines and thrown into the city of Caffa, so that by means of these intolerable passengers the defenders died widely … What seemed like mountains of dead were thrown into the city, and the Christians could not hide or flee or escape from them, although they dumped as many bodies as they could into the sea. Soon the rotting corpses tainted the air and poisoned the water supply … Moreover, one infected man could carry the poison to others, and infect people and places with the disease, by look alone.*

The range of a medieval siege engine, such as a cata-pult or trebuchet, was approximately 200 metres (660 feet). Human bodies could possibly have been hurled further. It didn't much matter, though, because the Mongols could aim anywhere in Caffa: their target was an entire city.

It is hard to imagine what it would have been like to have been one of the 70,000 inhabitants of Caffa at this time: looking up into the sky to see a tiny figure growing bigger and bigger until it is revealed as a twisting corpse, which then lands with a spray of body fluid on the street in front of your home. Thousands and thousands of corpses rained down on the city. Everywhere the inhabitants went, they would have had to have kept their eyes to the sky, watching for falling bodies, and they would have heard continual heavy thuds as the deadly bodies crashed to the ground.

And then the dying would have commenced. Professor Mark Wheelis, a microbiologist who has studied the siege of Caffa, thinks the disease would have spread quickly as city inhabitants, many of whom almost certainly would have had 'cut and abraded' hands, handled the torn-apart corpses, trying to drag them out of the way. As people in the town began to die, chaos would have set in. Based on the evidence of later plague outbreaks, the infected would soon have been left dying in the streets, to be devoured by animals, which would then have passed the disease on to more humans. In the meantime, hordes would have swarmed to the waterfront, the only way out of the ghastly town of Caffa, to try to beg, bribe or fight their way onto any seagoing transport available.

## A Deadly Cargo

By the spring of 1347, what was left of the Mongol forces abandoned Caffa and straggled back home. Any Genoese who could find a berth on a ship fled back to their home. It was a very long journey—more than 2500 kilometres (1500 miles)—first to Constantinople, then across the Mediterranean. No one knows how some of the infected travellers managed to survive that long—the only likely explanation is that some had hardier genes than others—but, in October of 1347, a fleet of ships carrying Genoese from Caffa reached Messina, in Sicily. Most of the crewmen were either dead or dying. Some ships washed ashore on the coast with no one on board left alive.

From Messina, the plague spread to Genoa and Venice, then to France, Spain, Portugal and Britain by 1349, before infecting Scandinavia, Germany and western Russia. It burned through Europe for the next three years, killing one-third of the population. Then it was gone, although cycles of plague would return, again and again over the next few centuries.

Biological warfare has taken many forms over the years, but few instances before the twentieth century have been as horrible as the infected cadavers smashing down on the streets of Caffa. It is certain that the plague would have reached Europe another way had the siege of Caffa not occurred, but it struck faster and with greater impact because of a Mongol khan's decision to hurl his corpses—dead men on a mission of vengeance—into the shining city of his Christian enemies.

# CHAPTER SIX

## The Snatch

## Francisco Pizarro kidnaps Inca King Atahuallpa, 1532

That November day in 1532, in the Inca town of Cajamarca, the odds were laughable: 168 Spanish conquistadors against 80,000 Inca troops. True, the Spanish had sixty-two horses, guns, and swords of steel, none of which the Inca—armed with wooden clubs, slings, bows and arrows, blowguns and spears—had ever seen before. And the conquistadors, whatever one might think of men who seek to destroy civilisations for the sake of gold, were brave. But this was too much, even for them. As the Inca ruler Atahuallpa—considered a god by his subjects—approached with his guard of 7000 warriors, the Spaniards, as a chronicler recorded, 'made water without knowing it, out of sheer terror'.

But the conquistador leader, Francisco Pizarro—second cousin to the more famous Hernán Cortés, conqueror of the Aztecs a decade before—had a trick up his sleeve. Pizarro was illiterate, untrustworthy and ruthlessly ambitious, but he was also cunning. In such a situation, the only tactic that made any sense from the point of view of the greatly outnumbered Spaniards was kidnapping, or, more colloquially, a snatch. In this case, the snatchee would have to be Atahuallpa himself, ruler of an empire that covered 32 degrees of latitude, making it, in 1532, the largest empire on earth.

Perhaps it would have been unwise for Francisco Pizarro to ponder just how large a chunk of the world he and his few score men were about to bite off—there are more pressing issues to deal with when you are outnumbered almost 500 to 1. But his actions would have larger consequences than most kidnappings, consequences that would include the decline of one empire and the rise of another.

### Fabled Cities of Gold

After landing on an island in the Caribbean in 1492, Christopher Columbus thought he had discovered a new route to the Indies. He had not. But he had found a world that would vastly enrich the Spanish masters for whom he sailed, putting them a step up in their race for global domination against the Portuguese and English. The first Spanish island possessions in the Americas—Cuba, Hispaniola and Puerto Rico—did not deliver much in the way of the gold that the Europeans treasured, nor did Panama, settled by its discoverer, Vasco Núñez de Balboa, in 1512. But rumours of golden cities in the Americas persisted; two of the favourite legends were of the Seven Cities of Cibola, thought to exist in North America, and El Dorado in South America, where even the fountains in the plazas were said to be made of the metal. The conquistadors—meaning 'conquerors', the soldiers of fortune who peopled the Spanish colonies—were, almost to a man, desperate to be the first to enter such a city. And in 1521, one of their number, Hernán Cortés, actually did so, conquering the fabulous city of the Aztecs in what is now Mexico, and enriching himself and Spain immeasurably.

Cortés' discovery—which, in a way, revealed that golden cities did exist—set off a race among conquistadors to be the first to discover another one. One keen competitor was Francisco Pizarro, who was actually a rather unlikely conqueror, as it happens. Born in 1475 in Trujillo, Spain, he was the illegitimate son of an infantry captain. Neither his father nor his mother wanted much to do with him—he was apparently never schooled and so was illiterate all his life. By the time he was twenty-two, he had sailed to Hispaniola, where he made a living herding pigs—the basis for many of the epithets hurled at Pizarro by his enemies, who were legion (Pizarro had his cousin Hernán's smarts and reckless courage, but not his charm).

Soon, however, Pizarro sought to enrich himself through adventure. He was with Balboa when the latter hacked his way across the Isthmus of Panama and discovered the Pacific Ocean in 1512. He was in Panama in 1522 when another conquistador, Pascual de Andagoya, returned from the very first exploration of the shores of western South America recounting tales of an unbelievably wealthy country far to the south, called Pirú or Virú. Andagoya had become sick and returned without actually seeing this country, but these rumours were all Pizarro needed to hear. As if sensing his destiny in these fabulous tales, he made preparations to sail south.

## The Land of Four Quarters

The Inca Empire, tucked between the Andes and the west coast of South America and covering much of modern-day Ecuador, Peru and northern Chile, was one of the best kept secrets of the early sixteenth century. It was a relatively new empire. The Inca tribe had taken shape around AD 1200, when a band of Indians from Lake Titicaca (on the border between present-day Bolivia and Peru) migrated south and founded the city of Qosqo (modern Cuzco) in the Andes. That the Inca thrived in this alpine environment, at heights of up to 4000 metres (13,000 feet), where slopes averaged a steep 65-per-cent incline and where extremes of weather were common, was extraordinary in itself—the Inca were obviously a hardy lot. But even more impressively, beginning about 1350, they pushed their way out of their mountains, conquering neighbouring tribes, until they reached the Pacific Ocean, and then moved north and south. In a series of empire-building moves worthy of the Mongols, the Inca eventually acquired territory that stretched for 4000 kilo-metres (2500 miles), from mountaintops to ocean.

In the Quechuan language of the Inca, their land was known as Tawatinsuyu, or 'The Land of Four Quarters', for the highly organised Inca had divided up their country into four different departments, or administrative districts, all ruled by the Inca, which in Quechua means 'lord' or 'royal person', from the capital city of Qosqo. To connect the different parts of their empire, the Inca put in 40,000 kilometres (25,000 miles) of stone roads. Everyone in the land of the Inca worked, at least part of the time, for the empire—building roads, making cloth, growing crops, mining guano on offshore islands or soldiering. The Inca practised relocation, moving conquered populations from one end of the empire to the other, if required. Some historians have even compared the Inca state to Soviet Russia: food and lodging were provided to all, but the masses were merely pawns in the games played by their rulers.

And what rulers they were. Ensconced in his fabled palace in Qosqo was the Inca himself, so all-powerful that even his bodily wastes and fingernail clippings were collected and saved by retainers. He was considered immortal, which led to an Inca custom that fascinated the Spanish: whenever an Inca died—of course, he hadn't *actually* died, given his god-like status, simply shifted into an altered eternal state—his corpse was mummified. Since the Inca used sophisticated embalming methods and since the high air of Qosqo is almost perfectly dry, the mummy lived on forever.

So the Inca capital was filled with mummy-corpses who ruled from their separate palaces, and had households full of relatives and retainers with their own political agendas. The place was as replete with intrigue as any Medici court, but it was all fomented by dead men. As Pizarro said: 'The greater part of the people, treasure, expenses and vices … were [*sic*] under the control of the dead'.

Controlled by the dead or not, the Inca world was a powerful one. By 1530, the empire had been at its fullest extent for about one hundred years. And then pale-skinned men arrived, unbidden, on its northern borders.

### Enter Pizarro

Francisco Pizarro was nothing if not dogged. He made three separate attempts to reach the land of the Inca in 1524, 1526 and 1528. Each time, he and his expedition were turned back by various hardships, including hunger, skirmishes with hostile tribes and incredibly arduous terrain. But on his third expedition, Pizarro managed to land briefly at Tumbes, in what is now northern Peru; there, he saw local Indians wearing decorations of gold and silver and learned that the Inca Empire was a reality.

Pizarro sailed back to Panama, and thence to Spain, where he showed Inca treasures to King Charles V, especially objects of worked gold and silver. He then received a charter to 'extend the empire of Castile'.

In 1530, Pizarro set forth with 168 men on his last expedition to the Andes. But when he arrived in Tumbes, he found the town empty and desolate. Tragically for the Inca (but quite fortunately for Pizarro), the empire had experienced two plagues: one was smallpox, which ravaged Inca civilisation in the mid to late 1520s; the other was civil war. The Inca ruler Huayna Capac had died in 1525, possibly of smallpox. Unfortunately, he had not appointed a successor. So his sons Huáscar and Atahuallpa began a bloody war to decide who would become Inca. In the summer of 1532, just before Pizarro and his men showed up, Huáscar and Atahuallpa fought a decisive battle in which Atahuallpa triumphed, leaving thousands dead on the battlefield. Huáscar was captured and sent as a captive to Qosqo.

Because of this great battle, Atahuallpa and his 80,000-strong army were still close to Tumbes when word of the arrival of a group of strange, pale-skinned men reached them. Atahuallpa was not overly concerned about such a small force, but the men were a curiosity he decided he wanted to see, and so he sent word that they were to meet him in the town of Cajamarca. Had Atahuallpa been in his high capital city of Qosqo, it is possible he might not have been so curious. It is also possible that, deep in the heart of the Inca Empire, Pizarro might not have attempted what he did.

### Rendezvous at Cajamarca

When Pizarro and his men received word that the Inca wanted to see them, they journeyed the short distance to Cajamarca, and there spent a nervous night awaiting his arrival. It was almost certainly during this restless evening that Pizarro came up with the idea of kidnapping Atahuallpa. In this, he may have been inspired by the example of his cousin Cortés, who had seized the Mexican ruler Montezuma II in a similar fashion. But Pizarro's situation, as he recognised, was even more precarious than Cortés', as he didn't have as many men, nor the Indian allies his cousin had recruited along the way. Pizarro warned his men that the slightest show of fear would cause the Inca to slaughter them. It was apparent to him that, in the face of the overwhelming number of Inca and with no prospect of any backup, the only way to turn the situation to their advantage was by a sudden, surprising and forceful move. And he set about devising a trap in which Atahuallpa himself would be caught.

Next day, 16 November 1532, Atahuallpa, brimming with confidence after his victory, showed up with his personal bodyguard of 7000 Inca warriors. He was carried into the square on a litter decorated with jewels and feathers, surrounded by eighty nobles who were his personal retainers. Other retainers swept the plaza before the litter, while the bodyguards roared songs in a language none of the conquistadors could understand. They understood the show of power, however, and were terrified, some of them even losing control of their bladders at this point, as one of their number recorded.

Cajamarca had a long central plaza surrounded on three sides by empty royal buildings. The Inca crowded the square, filling it to overflowing, while the Spanish lined the buildings on all three sides. From the start, the conquistadors sought to provoke Atahuallpa. Knowing that the Inca were terrified of horses—in fact, they thought them some mutated form of human being—the conquistadors pranced their steeds around the edges of the square.

## Defending the Faith

A friar, Father Vicente Valverde, who accompanied the conquistadors, was sent out by Pizarro to speak with Atahuallpa through an interpreter. He told the Inca that he must give up his cherished beliefs and become a Christian. When Atahuallpa asked the friar what gave him the right to ask this of him, Valverde handed him his Christian breviary, his book of daily prayers. Atahuallpa held it to his head, listened for a moment and then snorted. 'This book does not talk to me', he said, and he threw it on the ground. Whether Pizarro had actually planned this little scenario with Valverde or not, it played right into Spanish hands.

Valverde shouted that the Inca had insulted the Christian faith. At which point, responding to a signal prearranged by Pizarro, a trumpet blew, guns fired, a small cannon belched flame and the conquistadors charged from beneath the shelter of the buildings in the square. These unfamiliar sights and sounds sent the Inca into a panic. They trampled over each other in an effort to escape, smothering some of their number and leaving mounds of dead in the plaza. A slaughter ensued. The Spaniards hacked away with their steel swords and rode down the Inca with their horses. Not only were the Inca shocked by this brutal onslaught, but most of the warriors present had come with only ceremonial arms and were not able to defend themselves effectively.

The Spanish conquistadors killed thousands. Pathetically, the Inca clustered around the litter bearing Atahuallpa, trying to protect him as they were killed one by one. Some of them carried the litter on their shoulders, even after having their arms hacked off. Finally, Pizarro himself dragged Atahuallpa off the litter and made him captive. The immense Inca army stationed just outside the town joined the panicked bodyguards in flight after their ruler was snatched. One Spanish observer described the countryside around Cajamarca as being blanketed in all directions, as far as one could see, with retreating, terrified Inca.

### The End of an Empire

At first, the Spanish treated Atahuallpa well, giving him food and allowing certain of his retainers to see him. After a few days, he finally understood what these men wanted: gold. To the Inca and his people, this was absurd. Gold decorated their shrines and the statues of their gods, but had no value aside from the fact that it was pleasing to the eye. (The Inca essentially had no economy and did not use gold or silver as barter.) So Atahuallpa promised the Spaniards an entire room full of gold—7 metres (23 feet) by 5 metres (16 feet) by more than 2 metres (6½ feet) high—and another two rooms filled with silver, if they would let him go.

To this, Pizarro acquiesced. From December to May, cartloads of gold and silver made their way to Cajamarca, as the Inca stripped shrines of the precious metals. Meanwhile, Atahuallpa schemed. He sent word to his men to kill Huáscar, who was still a captive, and any of his other brothers who remained alive—he was trying to make sure that no one would conspire against him while he was imprisoned. Pizarro, in the meantime, waited for the gold to arrive and developed his own strategy. He familiarised himself with Inca society and politics and conspired with Tupac Huallpa, an ambitious half-brother of Atahuallpa. If Tupac would take an oath of fealty to Spain, Pizarro would have Atahuallpa killed and support Tupac as the new Inca. This would leave Pizarro with a friendly Inca rather than one who would almost certainly seek revenge.

The deal was made, and Atahuallpa's fate was sealed. Pizarro then offered him a choice: he could either be burned to death at the stake as a heretic or garrotted—the latter a mercy that would be given him only if he converted to Christianity. Faced with the fate of being burned, which would deny him immortal life as a mummy, Atahuallpa chose to be baptised, and was then garrotted in May of 1533.

With Tupac Huallpa installed as the new Inca, Pizarro then marched on Qosqo and assumed control of the region. Aided by smallpox, which had greatly weakened the empire, Pizarro had done what had seemed impossible: he had destroyed an entire culture and taken over a nation of 5 million people with a force of just 168 men.

The Inca would continue to resist Spanish rule through a guerrilla war that lasted forty years, but the outcome was never in doubt. Pizarro grew rich, but never gave up scheming. In 1541, he was shot dead in Lima by the son of a conquistador he had betrayed. As he died, he reached out a trembling finger and drew a cross on the floor in his own blood.

CHAPTER SEVEN

## Les Sauvages' Secret Weapon
### Champlain defeats the Iroquois, 1609

'**A** boundless vision grows before us; an untamed continent; vast wastes of forest verdure; mountains silent in primeval sleep; river, lake and glittering pool; wilderness oceans mingling with the sky.' Thus the great nineteenth-century American historian Francis Parkman described his vision of the country that opened up for French adventurers in the earliest days of European exploration of what was then called New France, and is now Canada. Parkman saw the beauty of this wild country with a romantic eye, but he was not blind to its dangers—for all its glory, New France was a 'churlish wilderness, [with] a pitiless climate', where, at any moment 'disease, misery and death' would fell the unwary.

New France was inhabited by Indians, whom the French invariably called *les sauvages*—'the savages', or, in other words, 'the uncivilised ones'.

These 'savages' were populous and had made their home there for centuries. When the French under the great explorer and empire-builder Samuel de Champlain arrived on the scene, the Indians of what is now eastern Canada—the Huron, Micmac and Algonquin, among others—were engaged in a bitter war with the Iroquois of present-day New York State—a group of allied tribes, including the Cayuga, Oneida and Mohawk, who all spoke Iroquoian languages and some of whom had set up the so-called Confederacy of Five Nations.

In one of those marriages of convenience that so often marked early North American history, the Canadian Indians and Samuel de Champlain combined forces. Champlain, hoping to gain the Indians' favour and thereby get them to guide him deeper into the interior of the continent, offered to help them defeat their enemies using his powerful firearms. The Indians, realising the potentially devastating impact of such weapons on the Iroquois—who had not seen white men, let alone faced their guns—agreed.

And so, on a July day in 1609, they delivered Champlain, hidden in the bottom of a canoe, covered with animal skins, to the site of a small battlefield on the shores of one of the 'wilderness oceans' Parkman wrote about, and North American history changed forever.

## An Inhospitable Land

The less hospitable northern part of the American continent took longer to feel the colonising touch of Europeans than the Caribbean, Mexico or South America. Although the Viking Leif Ericsson sailed from Greenland to discover Newfoundland in about AD 1000, it was a long time before John Cabot voyaged back there to claim it for England, in 1497. For decades after that, French and Portuguese fishermen came to harvest cod in the teeming coastal waters of Newfoundland, but never stayed more than a few weeks at a time.

In 1524, Giovanni da Verrazano, in the employ of the French king, voyaged as far as Newfoundland, but it was not until the three voyages of Jacques Cartier, from 1534 to 1541, that France made a real effort to build a colony that rivalled those of its enemy Spain, to the south. Cartier sailed along the St Lawrence River as far as present-day Quebec, where he twice tried, and failed, to build a permanent settlement. Although a great explorer, he became obsessed with finding a place called the Kingdom of Saguenay, a mythical land far to the north filled with gold and diamonds, and made a fool of himself in the process. His other signal failure was to instill hatred in the hearts of the Indians, who could have been his allies, by kidnapping some of them and taking them back to France. When Samuel de Champlain arrived in the wilderness of New France some sixty years later, he vowed not to make the same mistakes as Cartier.

Samuel de Champlain was born some time around 1570, in Brouage, a seaport town on the west coast of France, just south of Brittany. Relatively little is known of Champlain's early life, and the first record of him is as a soldier fighting in the French army of King Henry IV against the Spanish, in 1594. When the war ended four years later, Champlain signed on as a sailor with ships plying their trade in the West Indies.

Following at least six transatlantic voyages, he emerged a well-rounded figure: a brilliant sailor who wrote the widely read *Treatise on Seamanship*; a chartmaker so exacting that his maps can be followed today; an artist who sketched with proficiency all the extraordinary sights of his long life;

and a man who, though a warrior, was far more compassionate than most of his contemporaries to the indigenous peoples he encountered.

In 1603, Champlain sailed with a French company with instructions from King Henry IV to develop the existing fur trade with the Micmac, or Montagnais, Indians. Between 1604 and 1606, Champlain made several more voyages to New France with fur-trading groups chartered by the king to form monopolies. Given his own ship, he explored the American coastline as far south as Cape Cod, in present-day Massachusetts. He made charts, which he illustrated, sought places useful for trade or settlement, and, above all, studied the native people that he met.

The Indians were a bundle of contradictions. The men could spend days in energetic canoeing and hunting, but then might lie on their backs for a week, almost without moving, stuffing themselves with food until they became ill. They were incredibly obscene: their talk often resembled bawdy bar banter of today, and one of their favourite tricks was to stand outside of missile range, pull down their pants and moon their enemies. Yet they were, in their own way, extraordinarily spiritual. They believed in the power of dreams, and paid close attention to what those dreams seemed to foretell. For the Indians, the wilderness was not just trees, rocks and water, but a place where good and evil spirits dwelled, into which the dead disappeared after they died, and where voices could be heard whispering of the future.

The Indians may have been uncivilised from a French point of view, but they were not stupid. They refused Champlain's entreaties to take him further into the interior, to the source of the furs they traded. A frustrated Champlain went back to France and returned to North America, in July of 1608, with a company of thirty men and another charter from the king to seek out those elusive furs. He sailed up the St Lawrence to the site of modern-day Quebec (the name comes from the Micmac word *Kebec*, meaning 'the place where the river narrows') and built a habitation, a three-storey house surrounded by a moat, and tried to lay in food and crops for the winter. But, although he knew the cold weather could be severe, Champlain was unprepared for the terrible winter of 1608–09. By the time it was over, only eight of the twenty-four Frenchmen who had begun the winter there were alive, the rest having died of malnutrition and scurvy. Despite his lack of food, Champlain made it a point to feed a band of Micmac Indians who had crossed the St Lawrence on ice floes, so desperate were they to find food. The Indians were grateful for his kindness, but it was not enough to get them to help him explore westwards. Soon, however, Champlain came up with a plan.

In the spring of 1609, he offered to help the local Indians in their fight against the Iroquois if, in return, they would take him west, to the present-day Great Lakes. He pointed out to the hesitating chiefs that by employing his firearms—specifically, the arquebus, an early type of matchlock firearm—they could alter forever the balance of power between themselves and their traditional enemy. Finally, the chiefs, who had seen what the arquebus could do, assented.

### Advancing on the Iroquois

In the middle of June, the Hurons and Algonquins came from further west and north to join the Micmacs and form a great force of about 2000 Indians. Champlain led this army west on the river, sailing in a two-masted shallop while the Indians paddled in canoes against the St Lawrence's powerful current. They travelled through the Lake of St Peter, before finally reaching the mouth of the River des Iroquois, today known as the Richelieu River, which would take Champlain's battle force deep into Iroquois territory in northern New York State. Here, frustratingly, after a great feast and war dance festival that lasted two days, most of the allied Indians decided they didn't feel like fighting after all, traded some goods with their fellows and disappeared back into the woods.

Champlain proceeded anyway, but soon realised that he was faced with rapids so turbulent that his shallop would never be able to traverse them. Since the vessel was too heavy to portage, he sent it back to Quebec with most of his men, taking with him only two volunteers. The Indians who remained were only sixty strong, and they had twenty-four canoes among them.

Champlain travelled with his Indian allies until he reached the vast lake that today bears his name: Lake Champlain. To the west were the snow-capped Adirondacks. Early on the morning of 29 July, as they paddled their canoes along the shores of the lake, Champlain and the Indians saw dark shapes across the water: the canoes of the Iroquois. Both sides spotted each other at the same time, and began shouting insults, trying to outdo each other with offensive references to ancestors and scatological inventions. This went on for some time, Champlain drolly noted, for all the world like 'the besiegers and besieged in a beleaguered [European] town'. Finally, representatives of both forces met and decreed that the fight would take place on the shore, on the following morning.

### 'The Iroquois Were Much Astonished'

When morning came, Champlain and his allies looked across the lake to see the Iroquois waiting for them, brandishing their weapons. There were perhaps a hundred of them. Although Champlain had supplied the secret weapon, it was the Hurons who furnished the battle plan. They instructed Champlain and his two French companions to lie down in the bottoms of their canoes, and covered them with furs. Then they paddled the canoes across to meet the Iroquois, who were arrayed in a small meadow on a point of land where Fort Ticonderoga—a much-contested citadel in American history—would later be built.

When the canoes landed, the Hurons and their allies leaped out and arrayed themselves in a battle line. Then, at the behest of the Hurons, Champlain arose from his covering of furs. He was wearing a doublet and long hose, over which he had placed armour consisting of a breast and back plate, and cuirasses to protect his thighs, all made of steel. On his head he wore a helmet with a white plume.

Champlain ordered his two volunteers to crawl into the woods on the side of the meadow. Then he advanced behind his allies towards the enemy. The Iroquois were armed with bows and arrows and shields made of wood and hide. Their chiefs, who wore long white feathers in their headdresses, had previously been pointed out to Champlain as prime targets by the Hurons. The Canadian Indians now parted into two groups to let Champlain through. Champlain loaded his gun with four balls of lead and advanced until he was only 30 metres (100 feet) from the enemy. In a moment redolent with drama and significance, the Iroquois, Champlain wrote later, 'halted and gazed at me and I at them'.

When he saw them make a move to draw their bows, he aimed his arquebus at the chiefs and fired. Two Iroquois leaders fell dead, and another was mortally wounded. 'The Iroquois were much astonished', Champlain wrote, 'that two men could be killed so quickly', and that their thick shields, effective enough in warding off arrows, were no match for this flaming and explosive weapon. There followed an exchange of arrows, and then Champlain's compatriots fired their arquebuses from the woods. This so dismayed the Iroquois that they turned and fled.

### One Hundred and Fifty Years of Enmity

The shot from Samuel de Champlain's gun changed the face of warfare in North America. The Iroquois hurried to purchase arms from Dutch traders in New York. They remained not only enemies of the Hurons, Micmacs and Algonquins, but also became sworn foes of the French, as well. In the battles that would culminate in the French and Indian War of the mid eighteenth century, the Iroquois would side with the British.

In the short term, the victory boosted the fortunes of Champlain and his Indian allies. With their help, he would subsequently explore North America as far west as the Great Lakes, pioneering a lucrative empire for France until his death in 1635.

For the Hurons and their allies, the triumph was not a lasting one, but it was extremely satisfying. On the night after the battle, they took great pleasure in torturing and burning to death Iroquois prisoners. Champlain was horrified, and even insisted on the right to shoot one poor captive to put him out of his misery. Undeterred, the Indians cut off the arms and legs of one of the Iroquois Champlain had slain in the battle, and presented these grisly trophies to him—with the understanding that he would take them back to France and offer them to his king.

# CHAPTER EIGHT

# Turning Weakness into Strength
## The American victory at Cowpens, 1781

It lasted perhaps forty minutes, about the time it might take you or me to make a quick shopping trip or grab a sandwich with a friend. But in those forty minutes the course of the War of American Independence was changed.

The Battle of Cowpens took place on 17 January 1781, in common pasturing ground in rural South Carolina, and led directly to the epochal surrender of Lord Cornwallis' forces at Yorktown, Virginia, some ten months later, and, in turn, the beginning of the American nation. But Cowpens is also significant because it was won by a homegrown commander, Brigadier General Daniel Morgan, whose alignment of his Continental forces on the battlefield was brilliant, and harked back, albeit on a smaller scale, to Hannibal's double envelopment at Cannae (see p. 23). Morgan was a commander who stood common military wisdom on its head. He turned his enemy's strength against it, and turned his own troops' weakness to his advantage. As a result, as historian John Buchanan put it, he became 'the only general in the American Revolution, on either side, to produce a significant original tactical thought'.

### Revolution in the South

Most of the early phase of the War of American Independence, which began in 1775, was fought in the northern states, especially Massachusetts—the tinderbox that had sparked American discontent with British rule—New York and New Jersey. After initial defeats, American armies under Generals George Washington and Horatio Gates defeated the British at Trenton, New Jersey, and at Saratoga, New York, in 1777.

In 1778, General Sir Henry Clinton, the British commander, withdrew his forces to New York in order to preserve the army and protect the city against French naval power, France having just entered the war on the side of the Americans. Washington followed with his army, and a stalemate in the North ensued.

In the South, however, it was a different story. The British hoped to take advantage of the fact that the American regular army was much weaker there, and that a greater proportion of American civilians were Loyalists—or Tories, as they were called—and could be counted on to rally around the Crown. Clinton sent an expeditionary force from New York to Georgia in late 1778, which captured the city of Savannah with relative ease. After this success, Clinton himself, along with Major General Charles Cornwallis, set sail from New York with a large force of British regular army troops and captured Charleston, the region's biggest port. Cornwallis then shattered the forces of General Horatio Gates, sent south to do battle, at Camden, South Carolina, in August of 1780.

By December of 1780, the Continentals had been driven out of South Carolina and were regrouping in Charlotte, North Carolina, under Gates' replacement, the very capable General Nathanael Greene, who had been sent by George Washington to try to salvage the depressing situation. Greene's ragtag army of perhaps 2000 regular soldiers had little to eat, clothing inadequate for winter weather and little hope left after a series of bloody setbacks.

Prefiguring the conflict that would take place in the South eighty years later, the fighting in South Carolina had the vicious, psychotically violent, extremely personal nature of a civil war. While the professional armies might clash on the battlefield, militias belonging to the Loyalists and the Patriots fought impromptu skirmishes, after which prisoners could expect to be hung or hacked to death with sabres. Women and children were murdered in midnight raids, homes burned to the ground, politics used as a means to settle old scores.

Into this terrifying mix came the dashing figure of twenty-six-year-old Major Banastre Tarleton, commander of the British Legion, which was made up primarily of British Loyalists recruited in the North and trained exactingly by Tarleton and a small core of British army officers. Brave, impulsive and quite brutal, Tarleton was Cornwallis' right-hand commander, responsible for clearing American armies from South Carolina in a series of forceful fights at places like Monck's Corner, Lenud's Ferry and Fishing Creek, whose names give a sense of their isolation, deep in rural valleys. An incident during which Tarleton's men slaughtered a defeated and helpless American force at Waxhaws,

North Carolina, resulted in the British commander becoming known among the Patriots as 'Butcher' Tarleton, or 'Bloody Ban'. The phrase 'Tarleton's Quarter!' became a sneering and ironic reference to the mercy Americans intended to offer the British when next they met. They would soon have their opportunity, at Cowpens.

### 'To Spirit up the People'

Nathanael Greene knew that if he kept his forces in the same place for too long, the superior British army could simply throw a noose around them and gradually tighten it. So he decided to take action first, and in mid December divided his troops. He himself, with the bulk of his force, would threaten the British in eastern South Carolina. Sent west with a force of 800 men was Brigadier General Daniel Morgan, whose orders were to 'take command in that quarter, to act offensively or defensively, to protect the country, spirit up the people, annoy the enemy [and] collect provisions and forage'. To 'spirit up the people' meant to show the flag, so that patriotic Americans would join forces to drive out the British; and, indeed, as Morgan went, more and more militia joined his forces.

Just as Banastre Tarleton was the face of the British forces in the South, so Daniel Morgan came to typify the Americans. Not a great deal is known about Morgan's early life except that he was born in New Jersey in 1736 and as a teenager moved to Virginia. There he got a job driving a wagon—hence his own self-applied nickname, 'The Old Waggoner'. His first experience with the British was at the age of twenty, when he was a driver for the British army during the French and Indian War, the North American theatre of the Seven Years' War (1756–63) between Britain and France.

A year or so later, Morgan and two fellow soldiers were attacked by Indians. The soldiers were killed and Morgan shot in the back of the neck, the bullet smashing his teeth and exiting just above his left lip, leaving a permanent, livid scar. The incident showed that Morgan—a solidly built, stocky, plain-spoken and rough-humoured man—could survive almost any hardship.

Soon after the War of American Independence began, he became famous for leading a group of backwoods riflemen in fighting in Canada and at Saratoga. By 1781, after a leave of absence for health reasons, Morgan became a brigadier general commanding Greene's 'light troops'—a strike contingent comprised of regular soldiers, militia, dragoons (mounted infantry) and cavalry.

### In Hot Pursuit

As far as Cornwallis was concerned, Greene had made the cardinal military mistake of dividing his army in the face of a superior force; now he could be cut up, piecemeal. Accordingly, Cornwallis decided to send Tarleton after Morgan. Given two regular infantry companies in addition to his infamous British Legion (about 1100 men in all), Tarleton began to trail Morgan through the countryside in typically Southern winter weather—almost freezing, and raining much of the time.

However, every time Tarleton got within striking distance of Morgan, the latter withdrew, and Tarleton was forced to follow further and more aggressively. On the evening of 15 January, learning that Morgan was encamped nearby, Tarleton drove his men in an all-night march, which brought them so close to Morgan's forces on 16 January that the Americans were forced to abandon their breakfast and run for their lives. Sure now of an easy victory, the British marched all that day and then camped that night. Very early next morning, Tarleton's advance scouts came out of a pine forest to discover an American skirmish line arrayed at a place called Cowpens.

### A Counterintuitive Plan

On the afternoon of 16 January, Daniel Morgan, with the help of local scouts, finally arrived at the battleground of his choosing. Cowpens ('the cow pens') was a grazing area in the high pasture of South Carolina, which was used in common by the settlers in the area. About 500 metres (1650 feet) across and 500 metres (1650 feet) long, the land here was almost park-like: an open, sloping area dotted with trees where the undergrowth had been eaten away by livestock or cleared by farmers. The ground rose up in a gentle swell, and near the top of the slope there was a swale, or fold, in the land, just deep enough to hide a man on horseback.

Now Morgan began to do things that were brilliantly counterintuitive. Beyond the woods behind him, about 10 kilometres (6 miles) away, was the Broad River, which cut off the Americans' means of escape (an army attempting to cross a river under fire is an army inviting massacre). His chosed position thus violated a cardinal military rule—always give yourself an avenue of retreat. But Morgan did not want to provide his militia, which made up fully a quarter of his force, with a chance to retreat. For militia were notorious in the War of American Independence for always running away in the face of well-trained regular army troops, particularly if the latter employed bayonets. George Washington himself had gone on record to say that they were worse than useless.

Morgan planned to turn this 'uselessness' to his advantage. Understanding that these men would more than likely turn and run, he arrayed them as his first and second lines of defence: his skirmishers and his initial battle line. And then, *he gave them permission to run*.

Indeed, an eyewitness described how, the night before the battle, Morgan went among the militia, encouraging them and telling them that they were going to whip 'Benny' [Tarleton] handily the next day, and that all he needed them to do was, 'just hold up your heads, boys; three fires and you are home free, and then when you return to your homes, how the folks will bless you, and the girls kiss you, for your gallant conduct'.

The next part of Morgan's ingenious plan was to place his regular army soldiers—his third and last line of defence—in the bottom of the swale at the top of the slope. Conventionally, a commander would have placed them on the brow of the swale, looking down at the enemy, but Morgan wanted to keep these men hidden, to make the British think that the militia retreating before them represented the main force they faced.

Morgan also understood something vital about the mechanics of firing muskets and rifles in battle: men who fire downhill tend to fire too high, whereas men aiming uphill fire low and hit their targets more often. This was particularly true, the Americans had noted, of the British, whose muskets may have contained too much powder, which caused the bullet to fly higher than it ought to.

Morgan's flanks were protected on the right by a ravine and a small creek, and on the left by a swamp. In the woods directly behind his forces, he hid his cavalry and light dragoons commanded by Colonel William Washington.

There was one other factor on which his plan hinged, and on which he knew he could depend: Banastre Tarleton's aggressiveness.

## Tarleton Attacks

When Banastre Tarleton rode out of the misty woods at the head of his army on the morning of 17 January, he saw what he expected to see—a skirmish line of American scouts, and, further up the hill, what he assumed was the main body of the American forces. Without waiting to reconnoitre further, he formed his men into their usual attack formation: his legions and artillery (in this case, only two small field pieces which played little part in the subsequent battle) in the middle, and his dragoons on the flanks. A command was given and the men headed up the slope.

Almost at once, Morgan's skirmishers began firing. These men, sharpshooters mainly from the backwoods of the Carolinas and Georgia, armed with long rifles rather than the shorter-range, less accurate, smooth-bore muskets carried by most militia and Continentals, fired from about 150 metres (490 feet) in front of Morgan's initial battle line. Their job was to pick off British officers, and they may have killed about fifteen of the dragoons. When they were done firing their two (or three) shots, the skirmishers retired to the initial line, which opened to let them through.

At this point, the battle was proceeding just as Tarleton had expected—a typical display from the skirmishers, then a retreat to the main line. He now sent his infantry forwards in a broad charge along the whole front of the Cowpens pasture, heading straight at the militia.

On the American side, officers roamed behind their nervous men, encouraging them to hold their fire. Morgan himself was on the militia line, telling jokes and admonishing the men to 'squinney [aim] well and don't touch a trigger until you see the whites of their eyes'. When the British forces, moving at quick step, got within 50 metres (165 feet), Morgan screamed the order to fire, and the entire militia line erupted in smoke and yellow flame. The British line faltered, taking serious casualties, about 40 per cent of which were officers, but the well-trained men continued their attack. The militia fired again. Then they turned and ran as fast as they could up the slope.

The enraged British chased them, determined to wreak revenge for their dead and wounded. Most of the militia made it back to the protection of the back line (which had been ordered to open up to let them through), but one group of militia on the left of the Continental line were caught in the open by Tarleton's dragoons, who began to exact a fearful toll on the panicked men, cutting them down with flashing sabres. Witnessing this, William Washington's cavalry raced out of the woods and drove off the dragoons.

## Morgan's Triumph

Meanwhile, the main body of British troops, in three lines, their fifes playing and drums beating, continued to advance towards the last line of American defence, which was now apparent in the distance. Continental veterans of the battle later remembered Daniel Morgan everywhere among them, crying: 'Form, form, my brave fellows! Old Morgan was never beaten!'

The British crested the swale and aimed down at the American soldiers. Volley after volley of musket fire was unleashed by both sides—soldiers fired by company, rather than individually—at a range now of about 50 metres (165 feet); the bullets, said one participant, 'produced much slaughter'. Yet much of the British fire went high, as Morgan had predicted, while the Americans were able to aim up at British forces silhouetted against the skyline.

Instead of coming up against a line of Americans that cracked like the other two, the British now found themselves facing their strongest opposition of the day. They began to wither under the pressure. Observing this, Tarleton threw in his reserves, the Seventy-First Highlanders, who entered the battle to the unnerving shriek of bagpipes. Americans on the right flank misunderstood an order from their commander and began to retreat, with the British chasing them, but just as quickly Morgan rode up, turned the retreating Continentals around and had them fire a devastating volley into the pursing enemy at a range of 10 metres (33 feet).

Although this retreat and about-face had not been planned, it broke the British will. A moment later, Washington's mounted men swept in on the British right flank while the re-formed militia came in from the left. This double envelopment proved too much for the British, who began running or surrendering. Tarleton took a group of some forty Legion dragoons and made a charge to try to save the day, but it was too little, too late. Yelling 'Tarleton's Quarter!' the Americans swarmed over the British; it was only by the exercise of firm control on the part of Morgan's officers that a slaughter did not ensue.

## A Pivotal Victory

Tarleton and his battered forces made their way back to rejoin Cornwallis. They had lost 100 dead, more than 200 wounded and 600 prisoners. Morgan reported his total casualties as twelve dead and seventy-three wounded, though the real number of dead was probably closer to seventy. Morgan did not count the militia casualties since they were, technically, outside his command—not unnaturally, he wanted to make his victory seem even more impressive than it was. He needn't have feared. His victory was one of the most impressive of the war.

Not only that, despite being a relatively small battle, involving just 3000 or so combatants in all, Cowpens turned the tide of a stalemated war in the direction of the Americans and was a major psychological victory for the Patriots. In the next ten months, Greene carried on a campaign of attrition against Cornwallis, facing him on numerous battle-grounds after Cowpens and always, technically, losing—but in the end the British victories were hollow ones which cost them thousands of dead. Cornwallis was eventually cornered at Yorktown, Virginia, and forced to surrender in October 1781, bringing the war to an end.

Old Dan Morgan had retired by then—sciatica from a herniated disc made it nearly impossible for him to mount his horse—but he took great glee in his victory. As he wrote to a friend shortly after the Battle of Cowpens: 'I was desirous to have a stroke at Tarleton ... & I have Given him a devil of a whiping [*sic*]'.

# CHAPTER NINE

# The Prince of Deception
## John Magruder & the Peninsula Campaign, 1862

Even by the extremely colourful standards of the American Civil War—a war that included fighting circus acrobats, insanely brave cavalry officers, balloon aerialists and lady spies—Major General John Bankhead Magruder was a colourful figure. Over 190 centimetres (6 feet 3 inches) tall, dressed always in ornate uniforms, born with the gift of the gab—'he can talk twenty-four hours incessantly', a fellow officer complained—although also possessing an extreme lisp much parodied by his contemporaries, Magruder cut an extraordinary swath across mid-nineteenth-century America. 'The Prince', as he was known from his days at West Point onwards, made influential acquaintances ranging from Edgar Allen Poe and Thomas Jefferson to Abraham Lincoln and Emperor Maximilian I of Mexico.

Unfortunately, Magruder was also an alcoholic who wasted much of his promise and intellectual powers and was to die alone in a hotel room. But for a brief shining moment in the spring of 1862, a moment towards which his whole life seemed to have been aimed, he was in control of the tiny Confederate Army of the Peninsula which, thanks to Magruder's ingrained powers of drama and self-aggrandisement, managed to halt a far superior Northern army and save the day for the South.

## Unfulfilled Potential

John Bankhead Magruder was born in 1807 in Port Royal, in Virginia's Shenandoah Valley. Like many Virginians of the time, he grew up proud of the state's military tradition, which had provided several commanders in chief, as well as US presidents. Magruder went to the University of Virginia, where one of his fellow students was Edgar Allen Poe and where he dined with the ageing Thomas Jefferson. After that, he applied for and won a place at West Point, from which he graduated in 1830, before taking up a commission as a second lieutenant in the US Army. Although he came only fifteenth out of forty-two cadets in his West Point class, he had a reputation second to none as a man-about-town, a hard drinker and a larger-than-life personality. This was enhanced, a year after graduation, when he married a Baltimore heiress named Henrietta van Kapff, described by a friend of Magruder's as 'a weak woman, but good', of whom Magruder was fond, but whose wealth was also a decided attraction for a man on a meagre army pay.

With his personal magnetism, impressive intellectual powers and rich wife, Magruder could have gone far—as did fellow West Point classmates Robert E. Lee, Jefferson Davis and Joseph E. Johnston—but alcohol did him in. From the very beginning, he was a loud, dramatic drunk who would often black out in one city and find himself in another. So a career that might have been brilliant saw Magruder stay a second lieutenant for nearly thirty years, through postings to Florida, Maine, New York, Baton Rouge, San Diego and Mexico City.

Mexico was to save the Prince's career, for it was during the Mexican–American War in 1848, where he performed gallantly in action commanding a mounted light artillery unit, that he attained the rank of captain, and was even brevetted a lieutenant colonel (meaning that he was promoted temporarily for bravery, but without the pay commensurate with such a rank). It is typical of Magruder that he celebrated the army's victory and his personal achievement long and hard in Mexico City, forming something called the Aztec Club, a gaming and drinking group his fellow officers remembered fondly to the end of their days. It was also at the Aztec Club that Magruder got into a scrape with a fellow officer named Franklin Pierce, slapping him and sending his friend T.J. Jackson (later to be nicknamed 'Stonewall') to challenge Pierce to a duel. Fortunately, Pierce, who four years later became President of the United States, did not accept.

## A Southern Gentleman Goes to War

By 1861, Magruder (whose rank had reverted to captain) had knocked around more army posts and finally become commander of the garrison protecting Washington, D.C. His wife Henrietta, unable to stand his drinking and carousing, had taken their three children to Europe. With the Civil War about to break out, Magruder met personally with Abraham Lincoln and explained that, as a Virginian patriot, he was obliged to fight for the Rebel cause. (According to Magruder's somewhat suspect remembrance of the occasion, Lincoln accepted the loss with equanimity, complimenting Magruder for being 'a Southern gentleman'.) Then Magruder took a cab across a guarded bridge into Virginia and accepted a commission from his old classmate Jefferson Davis, then president of the Confederate States of America, as a major general in the Confederate Army. Among Magruder's fellow generals were Robert E. Lee and Joseph Johnston, his old West Point mates.

The war progressed badly for the Confederates at first, with the Union triumphing at Nashville and New Orleans. By late 1861, the high command at the Confederate capital of Richmond, Virginia, was aware that the Federals' next step would be an attempt to capture Richmond. And they knew where the invasion would come from: right up the historic peninsula of Virginia, formed by the York River on the north and the James River on the south.

With little in the way of alternatives, Jefferson Davis stationed Robert E. Lee to defend the city of Richmond, Joseph Johnston to guard the western approaches of the state, and Prince John Bankhead Magruder to command the 13,000-strong Army of the Peninsula.

## The Charade Begins

The new Union commander, General George B. McClellan, did exactly as the Confederates expected. But slowly. Despite his youth, the thirty-five-year-old was a plodding soldier who hated to move until he thought everything was in his favour. He spent the whole of the winter and early spring of 1862 gathering his forces at Fort Monroe, at the tip of the peninsula. Opposing him, John Magruder placed his 13,000 men in two lines across the peninsula. The first was a thin line about 20 kilometres (12 miles) from Fort Monroe, a line that was intended only to briefly halt the Yankees. The second was anchored at Yorktown in the north and the James River in the south, and ran along the line of the twisting Warwick River.

Because he had nowhere near enough men or materiel to populate the line, Magruder had to improvise. In this, he was in his element. While stationed in Corpus Christi, Texas, prior to the Mexican–American War, he had constructed an 800-seat theatre, created scenery and directed plays performed by the soldiers under his command, so he knew a little something about the magic of performance. He dammed the Warwick to create flooded areas in front of his defensive lines, cut down huge trees and had them sanded down, painted black and assembled as 'Quaker guns'—logs posing as cannon. He also instructed his officers on the art of 'diversion by marching'. Any large army creates a great deal of noise and movement, since in the natural course of business, men, horses and materiel shift from one place to another on a regular basis. So Magruder told his officers to keep his men marching back and forth, constantly, often dragging covered supply wagons (filled with wood or rocks). Some of his men didn't understand what he was up to—'Gen. Magruder is always drunk and giving foolish and absurd orders', wrote one soldier in his diary—but there was method in his madness.

## McClellan on the March

On Friday, 4 April, General George McClellan finally moved his 65,000 men towards Yorktown. As it marched west from Fort Monroe, the army divided into two columns, the northern column, on the right, heading for Yorktown, the southern column, on the left, aiming to sweep past and come up on Yorktown's flank. That first day, things went better than even McClellan could have hoped. The line of

Confederate soldiers in front of him (Magruder's first line of defence) simply vanished before the onslaught of Union forces.

The next day, however, was a bit different. Not only did it begin to rain, revealing to Union forces that the previously firm-seeming roads of the peninsula were covered with thin layers of topsoil that quickly turned to knee-deep mud, but, to McClellan's astonishment, he encountered a second line of defence that ran, not just around Yorktown, which was to be expected, but all across the waist of the peninsula. As one startled Union soldier subsequently wrote, 'We saw across an open space a long line of rebel earthworks with a stream in front; the rebel flag was flying and we could see secesh [secessionist] officers riding along their lines inside the works'.

The 'stream' was in fact the Warwick River. McClellan had thought it would be a mere trickle, but now, somehow, it represented a formidable obstacle. Not only was it swollen as a result of the rain, but also the Union commander began to receive reports from up and down his line that part of the river was comprised of large ponds—the result of Magruder's damming.

On 5 April, as his soldiers stared from their earthworks at the massive enemy force five times the size of theirs, Magruder gave a ringing speech of encouragement to his troops, then telegraphed Robert E. Lee in Richmond that the enemy was on the march. He told Lee the truth: 'I have made my arrangements to fight with my small force, but without the slightest hope of success'.

There was nothing for Magruder to do now but set his grand deception in motion.

## Conjuring up an Army

While the Yankee officers and men were watching his line, Magruder took a force of approximately 6000 troops, split them in half and sent them marching up and down behind his lines in two groups. The Yankees could just see them moving through gaps in the woods behind the Confederate works. Occasionally, one column or the other would flock to a point on the defences, as if to man it. Once concealed behind the battlements, most of them would sneak back along trenches, hidden from the enemy, into the trees, and then resume their marching up and down within sight of the Yankees. One Alabama trooper wrote: 'We have been travelling most of the day, seemingly with no other view than to show ourselves to the enemy at as many different points … as possible'. By repeating these operations over and over, Magruder managed to create the impression that a sizable force was concealed in the woods.

Whenever the Yankees ventured close to the Confederate defences, the Southerners responded with ferocious fire that not only kept the Yankees away, but also convinced them that there were a good many aggressive enemy soldiers manning the works. While all this was going on, Confederate soldiers hidden in the woods produced sounds that also enhanced the impression of a massive military force: yelling (of the infamous Rebel yell), shouting of orders, playing of bugles, pounding of drums, firing of muskets. Magruder's infamous 'Quaker guns' poked their wooden snouts out amid the real artillery, greatly amplifying Union fears of a slaughter if they decided to make a frontal assault.

Magruder's deception successfully brought the Federal forces to a halt, but life during the ensuing month-long stalemate was not easy for anyone. Torrential rains turned trenches into mud pits. Rations were short on the Confederate side, where the men existed on flour and beef jerky. The Union army employed a contingent of sharpshooters who fired at anything that moved, even African-American slaves delivering ammunition to Rebel trenches. At the same time, artillery shells burst repeatedly on both sides, taking a daily toll.

Meanwhile, in one of the first instances of balloons being used for observation in the Civil War, McClellan began sending 'Professor' Thaddeus S.C. Lowe, Chief Aeronaut of the Balloon Corps, aloft to observe the Confederate lines. Whenever this happened, Magruder kept his troops on the move, and directed his artillerists to fire at the balloon, forcing Lowe to remain at a distance and thus rendering his observations inaccurate.

As time went on, reinforcements, sent by Joseph Johnston, steadily poured in. By early May, Magruder's army numbered 33,000, a respectable force, though still nowhere near McClellan's numbers. In a move to unify his command, President Jefferson Davis combined Magruder's Army of the Peninsula with Johnston's force. The joined troops became known as the Army of Northern Virginia, with Johnston as overall commander. Magruder was far too junior in rank to expect to be given this command, but he may have been disappointed by Davis' actions, and his drinking increased. Despite this, he was the hero of the moment for the South. 'It was a wonderful thing, how he played his ten thousand before McClellan like fireflies and utterly deluded him', wrote Mary Chestnut, the Richmond diarist.

### A Brilliant Success?

After a month, McClellan brought up his huge siege guns from Fort Monroe and all was made ready for a grand offensive that was to begin on 5 May. On the night of 3 May, however, the Confederate lines opened up with a huge artillery barrage, using all of their heavy guns. The surprised Yankees kept their heads down, which was just what the Confederates wanted. When Professor Lowe went up again in his balloon on the morning of 4 May, he discovered that the Confederate works were empty. The entire Confederate army had retreated.

'Our success is brilliant', McClellan wrote, confident that his actions had caused the enemy to 'run away'. Others in the Union high command, including President Lincoln, were not so sure. McClellan had had the Confederates within his grasp and had taken a month to even begin a serious attack on them. And it wasn't as if Joe Johnston was defeated—he had simply withdrawn his army to more defensible positions around Richmond.

The retreat, however, was the beginning of the end of the glory days for John Magruder. During the subsequent weeks of fighting—which saw Robert E. Lee take over command of the Army of Northern Virginia after Joe Johnston proved too defence-minded—Magruder began taking morphine in addition to alcohol, possibly as a buffer against some of the dreadful sights he was seeing, for the fighting was the fiercest of the war to date. At the battles of White Oak Swamp and Malvern Hill, he seemed confused; at the latter battle, he ordered a futile attack after reading an outdated order from General Lee. This was not entirely his fault, but common sense and a clear head might have stopped an unnecessary loss of Confederate life.

Magruder was not a coward, as some charged. But his intake of alcohol and drugs, combined with stress and lack of sleep, caused him to make poor decisions. Even in a war noted for heavy drinking on both sides, his 'purplish, swollen veins' (as his aide described them) and air of being continually drunk or suffering from the effects of alcohol did not go unnoticed. In late 1862, after Robert E. Lee had defeated McClellan on the peninsula, Magruder was relieved of his command and sent to fight in the more remote western theatre of the war. There he partially redeemed his reputation by capturing the port city of Galveston, Texas, from the Yankees.

### The Last Days of Magruder

After the Confederate surrender in the spring of 1865, Magruder fled to Mexico, where he was hired by Emperor Maximilian I as a major general in the Mexican Army (numerous ex-Confederates took this route, forming a kind of expatriate colony). But after the forces of the Austrian-born emperor were defeated in May of 1867 and Maximilian executed, Magruder returned to the United States, where he was forced to take an oath of allegiance to the Union and was then pardoned.

He was sixty years old, without family and nearly penniless, yet, with typical aplomb, he managed to make a life for himself by travelling and giving lectures, not on his peninsula display, but on Mexico and Emperor Maximilian. However, by 1870, as a result of his advanced alcoholism, this means employment had ended. Magruder was forced to move to Houston, where he was supported by a former aide-de-camp who provided him with a stipend and a room in a hotel. It was there that John Magruder died alone, on 19 February 1871.

By no means was John Bankhead Magruder the most distinguished general the South ever produced, and it is true that his charade at Yorktown was aided by the excessive caution of George McClellan (indeed, Joe Johnston gruffly remarked, upon viewing Magruder's embattlements, 'no one but McClellan could have hesitated to attack'.) But the Prince's extraordinary deception in defence of his beloved Virginia is one of the most fascinating episodes in the annals of the American Civil War.

# CHAPTER TEN

# Horns of the Zulus
## The Battle of Isandhlwana, 1879

The great Shaka, founder of the Zulu Empire of the early nineteenth century, was, quite probably, a psychopath. He thought of killing human beings the way you or I might think of swatting flies on a summer's day. Once he became the ruler of the Zulus, he walked everywhere with executioners who, at a flick of his finger, would club or stab someone to death—for sneezing, not bowing low enough or simply looking the wrong way at the wrong time. When Shaka's mother, Nandi, died, he declared a year of mourning and summoned 20,000 of his Zulu citizens to his kraal, or village. He ordered that no crops be grown or children conceived for an entire year. Then a week of enforced grieving ensued. If someone was found without tears, he or she was executed. According to a European present, about 7000 people were thus massacred in a few days.

There are some who feel that these incidents are greatly exaggerated or invented by Europeans who must find a way to turn Africans into savages, but evidence indicating Shaka's brutality, even allowing for the culture in which he was brought up, seems overwhelming. But proof also exists for another, incontrovertible fact: that Shaka was a military genius whose innovations changed the face of warfare in Africa. Growing into manhood in the late eighteenth and early nineteenth centuries, without ever having met a white man or studied military science, he came up with an original way of fighting that perfectly suited his army, made Zululand a powerful nation and gave it the tools, long after his own death, with which to inflict an epic defeat on Great Britain, at the Battle of Isandhlwana in 1879. Soon after, the massed firepower of the 'civilised' world brought the Zulus to a halt, dead on the ground beneath their shields; but had Shaka still been around, who knows what would have happened?

## The Evolution of Bantu Warfare

The Zulu homeland, now encompassed by the South African province of KwaZulu-Natal, borders on the Indian Ocean in southeastern Africa. Zulus are members of the Bantu nation, a nomadic, cattle-driving race who probably arrived in central Africa from the Middle East over 10,000 years ago. Eventually, after perhaps 1000 years of wandering, the Bantu spread south and west and finally down into the southeastern part of the continent, pushing the original inhabitants of the region, the Bushmen, before them. The first European settlers of South Africa, the Dutch emigrants known as the Boers (Dutch for 'farmers'), also pushed the Bushmen out as they moved northeast over the course of a hundred years, beginning in the mid seventeenth century.

Neither Boers nor Bantu were aware of each other until they collided in the valley of the Great Fish River, in the late 1700s, each on their own separate migration. As the races collided, vicious fights and border skirmishes took place, a series of conflicts known as the Cape Frontier Wars. While this was going on, the British seized South Africa from the Dutch in 1794, inheriting a rich land and, eventually, a lot of trouble.

In the meantime, approximately 500 kilometres (300 miles) to the northeast, the Zulu tribe developed. The Zulus were part of a splinter group of Bantus, the Nguni, who had headed all the way into present-day KwaZulu-Natal and settled in the fertile area near the White Mfolozi River. The first chief, whose name was Zulu, which means 'the heavens', was followed by three brothers. The third brother, Senzangakona, fathered a child out of wedlock with a neighbouring chief's daughter, Nandi. Since she did not have the status of bride, Nandi tried to claim that her pregnancy was really an illness caused by a shaka, an intestinal beetle, and thus, when her son was born in about 1787, this was the name he was given.

As an illegitimate, barely acknowledged son of a king, Shaka was subjected to ridicule as a youth—ridicule for which he later took ferocious revenge. By the age of twenty-four, he had become a much-feared warrior working for a chieftain to whom the Zulus paid tribute. Much of Bantu warfare at this point consisted not of pitched battles, but of relatively bloodless skirmishes in which insults were exchanged and spears thrown from a distance. But the tactics of the chieftain, whose name was Dingiswayo, were more brutal: Shaka was involved in deadly battles in which Dingiswayo sought to capture slaves and take territory.

Young Shaka did not invent this kind of warfare among indigenous Africans, as is often claimed, but, as a commander appointed by Dingiswayo, he perfected it. To begin with, he changed himself. Deciding that he did not need sandals, he toughened his feet by going barefoot everywhere, no matter what the terrain. (Ultimately, Shaka ensured his soldiers could run barefoot as much as 80 kilometres [50 miles] a day and he made them practise on ground littered with thorns; those who winced or complained were executed.)

Shaka then modified the basic Zulu weapon of war: the spear. Prior to Shaka, the spear was used like a javelin, for throwing from a distance, which Shaka found absurd: once it was gone, you could not get it back and it was often turned against you. Shaka developed a shorter, flat-bladed stabbing spear, with a heavier handle, called the assegai by Europeans (but known far more descriptively in the Zulu language as the *ikwa*, for the sound the blade made as it was pulled out of a human body). Zulus carried several of these, which could be thrown if necessary at short range, but they always kept the last one for thrusting. Shaka also refined the Zulus' wood and cowhide shield, cutting it down in size so that it could be carried more easily in battle. Shaka showed his men how, in a fight, they could hook the shield under their opponent's larger shield, knock it out of the way and at the same time sweep in for the kill with the assegai. (At which point, Shaka always shouted 'I have eaten!', a phrase taken up by all Zulu warriors after blooding their spears.)

Shaka was allowed to train an *impi*, or regiment, this way and it proved highly effective. What's more, a few years later he developed the brilliant innovation that would become his most powerful and influential strategy: the *impondo zankomo*, or 'horns of the bull'.

## A Shape in the Sand

The Zulus were a people in love with their cattle. Everything revolved around these animals. Wives were bought with cattle, wealth measured by cattle, almost every need of the Zulus, from clothing to the milk curds that were a staple of their diet, was provided by cattle. So it was Shaka's genius to design a military manoeuvre based on the very form of these animals—a strategy that could be represented by a picture of a bull drawn in the sand and would easily be understood and appreciated by any Zulu.

Although it hadn't been his innovation, the Zulu regiment, or *impi*, was central to his plans. The *impi* could vary in size, having no precise number of men; in the beginning, Shaka's *impis* probably included no more than a hundred men each and possibly far fewer. In Shaka's plan, the main and strongest *impi* became the 'chest' of the bull, the main line facing the enemy. Behind it was a reserve force, which formed the bull's 'flanks' and was ready to be called into action if needed. On either side of the chest was Shaka's most important innovation, 'the horns'. The left and right horns, each consisting of one *impi*, raced out as the chest was moving forwards, flanking the opposing army and meeting behind it. If all worked according to plan, horns and chest met, surrounding the enemy and crushing it.

After a long period of training, Shaka put his strategy into effect one day around 1817. Fighting against a tribe that had persecuted him and his mother—and which was led by his half-brother—Shaka aligned his forces and attacked. The fast-moving horns of the bull swept behind the enemy, while Shaka and the main body of his men made short work of the opponents in front of them. Shaka then killed his half-brother and ruthlessly executed every member of the enemy clan, including all the women and children.

### Shaka's Assassination

By about 1819, Dingiswayo having been murdered by a rival chief, Shaka took control of the Zulus and led them to victory after victory, using the 'horns of the bull' tactic repeatedly. His force grew to as many as 20,000 warriors—after every victory, the enemy soldiers who remained were trained by Shaka's commanders and absorbed into the Zulus.

By 1824, Shaka had conquered all the tribes and clans within a territory that stretched from the Indian Ocean west to the Kalahari Desert, north to Lake Malawi and south to the Cape. He ruled brutally, but as effectively as any Ottoman or Mongol king; he was unimpeachable and seemingly unassailable.

Around 1824, he discovered a small British settlement at Port Natal and, out of curiosity, invited a party of Britons to visit him at his royal hearth, a kraal with the welcoming name of *kwaBulawayo*, or 'the place of him who kills'. While these visitors were in attendance, there was an attempt on Shaka's life by members of a neighbouring tribe. Shaka survived, in part because one of the Britons nursed him back to health. Because of this, he became well disposed to the white men and signed an agreement leasing them a large amount of territory around Port Natal (present-day Durban).

This one instance of benevolence from a brutal ruler turned out to be a great mistake from the Zulu point of view. In 1828, there was another assassination attempt on Shaka's life, by his two half-brothers, Dingane and Mhlangana, and this one succeeded. Bleeding from numerous wounds, Shaka pleaded with his killers to spare him, but they ruthlessly eviscerated him with the very assegais he himself had invented.

## An Unreasonable Ultimatum

Dingane immediately assassinated his brother Mhlangana and assumed the Zulu throne, instituting a pogrom against pro-Shaka family and chiefs that lasted several years; even so, his reign was far less bloody than that of Shaka. His main battles were with the Voortrekkers, those Boers who had decided to escape British rule and trek into the interior of South Africa and Natal. Dingane double-crossed and massacred many of them, but the

Voortrekkers beat off a major Zulu attack at Blood River, mainly through the use of modern firepower which included at least one cannon. Dingane was murdered and another half-brother, Mpande, ascended the throne just as the British moved in and took over Natal from the Boers in 1840.

Mpande and the British managed to coexist peacefully for a time, although there was internal dissension—as always—within the Zulu nation. However, in 1856, Mpande's two sons fought one of the most brutal conflicts in South African history, involving more than 50,000 Zulu warriors. Prince Cetshwayo won and slaughtered his brother's supporters by the thousands. Old King Mpande subsequently ruled as a figurehead, but Cetshwayo was the true power of Zululand and ascended the throne in 1872.

He was careful to cultivate good relations with the British, even going so far as to make sure his position as King of the Zulus was recognised by Queen Victoria. But the peace did not last long. Cetshwayo was continually skirmishing with the Boers who had settled in Transvaal, bordering Zululand in the north. At first, the British encouraged Cetshwayo, but once they took over Transvaal from the bankrupt Boers, they saw things very differently. A commission headed by Sir Henry Bartle Frere sided with the Boers on boundary issues and provoked the Zulus into a number of minor infringements. After the British issued a deliberately unreasonable ultimatum to Cetshwayo (telling him he must disband his army, among other things), they declared war and invaded Zululand at the beginning of 1879.

### The Ghost of Shaka

The British entered Zululand in three separate columns on 11 January 1879. All told, British forces numbered 5700 white troops and 8000 Africans. Their plan was to converge in three directions on the Zulu capital of Ulundi. Facing them were about 40,000 Zulu warriors. The British, under the command of Lieutenant General Frederic Augustus Thesiger, Lord Chelmsford, thought that superior British firepower, which included artillery as well as Gatling guns (forerunners of the modern machine gun), would easily win the day.

They had not bargained on the ghost of Shaka. Although some Zulu tactics and strict Zulu army discipline had been abandoned by the rulers who had succeeded Shaka, Cetshwayo had resurrected the king's militant ways. Every male over the age of sixteen was trained as a soldier. The Zulu army had been structured around twelve corps, with each corps made up of regiments segregated according to marital status and age—men as old as sixty still fought.

The Zulus had acquired some ancient muskets, though they still relied mainly on the assegai and were generally suspicious of firearms (some Zulus thought that bursting artillery shells contained British soldiers who leaped out of the explosion, and so could be seen spearing at the ground after shells burst among them). They also retained the 'horns of the bull', and the tactic was now worked on an even larger scale than in Shaka's day, creating a massive encircling movement that would take place over large tracts of ground and end up with the enemy caught in a bloody trap. As the British were about to find out.

### The Hidden Horn

On 21 January 1879, a portion of the central British column pitched its camp near the small mountain of Isandhlwana, just past the Buffalo River. The

British were approximately 1700 strong, including about 400 African auxiliaries, and were supported by artillery and rockets. Under the command of Lieutenant Colonel Henry Pulleine, the men did not entrench, perhaps owing to an overestimate of their strength, but they did pick what appeared to be an ideal spot from a conventional military viewpoint: they had their backs to the sheer rock face of Isandhlwana and in front of them was a broad and extensive plain, seemingly empty.

In the early afternoon of 22 January, however, British scouts on horseback reconnoitring a few kilometres in front of the British positions, found a large ravine hidden from sight on the plain. Peering over the edge of the chasm, they saw an astonishing thing: sitting in perfect silence, as far as the eye could see, were 20,000 Zulu warriors. Seeing the British, the Zulus arose as one. The scouts rode in a frenzy back to their camp as the Zulus began to come up over the edge of the ravine and across the plain.

Thus alerted, the British troops, which included two battalions of the experienced Twenty-fourth Warwickshire Regiment, formed an extended line to oppose the challenge of the onrushing Zulus.

At first, they were unconcerned; in fact, some of them were even laughing and chatting, happy in the knowledge that, finally, they were about to have their chance to bag some of the enemy. They might not have been so sanguine if they had been aware of the plans the Zulus had made for their destruction.

Interestingly, King Cetshwayo had decided the British could not be defeated in the traditional way and wanted to besiege them, but his generals had ignored him. They opted to use the age-old method of Shaka, but in a far grander way. At Isandhlwana, the 'chest' of the bull extended for 8 kilometres (5 miles). As these main troops began to run at the British positions at a slow speed, the younger and faster men who made up the horns began their encirclement. Here, too, there was a refinement: the Zulu commanders sent out their left horn in plain sight of the British defenders, but kept the right horn hidden in the distance. It slipped behind the flank of Isandhlwana, and the defenders knew nothing of its existence until the Zulus fell upon the wagon trains at their rear, slaughtering everyone in sight.

The British, who were familiar with the 'horns of the bull' tactic, but had not thought that it could be employed on such a vast scale, fought valiantly, beating off wave after wave of Zulus until their overextended line was overwhelmed. After two hours or so, almost the entire British contingent—1300 officers and men—had died, along with hundreds of black auxiliaries. About fifty-five British troops managed to escape, most of them wearing blue coats, because, for some reason, King Cetshwayo had told his men to concentrate on killing British soldiers wearing red coats. Up to 3000 Zulu warriors lay dead among them.

### Britain Finds an Answer

The Anglo–Zulu War lasted six months but was as savage as it was brief. Straight after Isandhlwana, the Zulus attacked British forces camped nearby at Rorke's Drift (a shallow river crossing) but these soldiers, forewarned, had barricaded themselves and were able to slaughter the Zulus, who advanced in wave after wave, with superior firepower. Finally, at the Battle of Ulundi that July, the British army formed a hollow square, supported by artillery and Gatling guns, and sent 12,000 Zulus reeling back, having finally discovered a way to defeat the 'horns of the bull': by firing a vast amount of ammunition—in this case, an estimated 35,000 rounds.

The war cost the Zulus their nation and around 10,000 lives. Afterwards, under British administration, they endured misery and chaos, civil war, famine and disease. There was just one small consolation: the Zulus could take pride in the fact that they had handed the British their worst defeat in Africa and one of their worst defeats of the entire colonial era.

# CHAPTER ELEVEN

## Kitchener's Gamble
### The Battle of Omdurman, 1898

Field Marshal Horatio Herbert Kitchener, First Earl Kitchener, more commonly known as Lord Kitchener, was not one of those commanders you could think of, by any stretch of the imagination, as beloved. People who knew him spoke of him as ruthless, forbidding and stern. If you doubt it, just take a look at his picture on one of the most famous military recruiting posters of all time, the First World War–era 'Lord Kitchener Wants You!' advertisement, in which he is depicted pointing a sternly admonitory finger at any nonmilitary men who might be shirking their way down the street. Enough to make you jump into uniform, just to escape his steely gaze.

On top of this, Kitchener was described as 'machine-like' in his decision-making, and such a micromanager that, while still a field commander, he refused to employ a chief of staff, making even the most insignificant decisions himself. He had little personal life and never married, although he was engaged for a time to a woman who died of typhoid fever in Cairo. Modern historians have spent many thousands of words speculating that Kitchener—with his love of ceramics and flowers—was gay and that he had an affair with his long-time aide-de-camp Captain Owen Fitzgerald, but he was probably more interested in work than love.

This dedication to his command resulted in some impressive achievements. Not the least of these was his extraordinary success in the Sudan at the Battle of Omdurman, where he headed a force that destroyed Islamic power in the region. The bloody fight at Omdurman is in itself a remarkable tale, but the way Kitchener got to that Muslim stronghold was an extraordinary physical as well as tactical achievement.

## Defying the Mahdi

The Sudan is the huge area south of Egypt and the Red Sea, traversed by the White and Blue Nile rivers, which join at Khartoum to form the Nile. In area, Sudan is today the tenth largest country in the world; nine other countries touch its borders. For centuries, it was known for trading in ivory and slaves. In 1820, Muhammad Ali, ruler of Egypt, conquered the country and its population of Islamic tribesmen and Coptic Christians. When Egypt became a British colony in 1882, the new rulers inherited this vast region with its imposing landscapes: dry deserts in the north, swamps and rainforests in the south, endless flat plains and jagged mountain ranges.

Just as Britain was taking over, a large faction of the Sudanese were in rebellion because Egypt had been trying to abolish the country's lucrative slave trade. The leader of the rebels was one Muhammad Ahmad ibn 'Abd Allah, a Sunni Muslim holy man who styled himself the Mahdi, 'Divine Holy One'. The Mahdi and his holy army (forerunners of today's jihadists) had destroyed the Egyptian army and were in the process of retaking the entire country. When the British sent in Major General Charles Gordon to evacuate the remaining Egyptian forces in 1885, he was surrounded in Khartoum and killed.

The Mahdi himself was killed in the summer of 1885, but the outnumbered British force in Egypt effectively ceded control of the Sudan to the

Mahdi's successor, the Khalifah ('deputy') 'Abd Allah, despite popular outcry in Britain to avenge Gordon's death. The dervishes of the Mahdist cause—the term was almost universally applied to the soldiers of the Mahdi and the Khalifah, although strictly speaking, a dervish is an ascetic Sufi holy man—attempted to invade Egypt, but the British pushed them back and then left them alone. By the mid 1890s, however, Lord Salisbury, the British prime minister, had become concerned that the growing militant Islamic power of the Mahdists would cause an uprising in other Muslim parts of the British Empire, such as India. This, along with a fear that Islamic Sudan might ally itself with the French, or even interfere with British access to the Suez Canal, which had been built in 1869, caused Salisbury to plan a British invasion of the Sudan.

## Kitchener, at Your Service

Horatio Herbert Kitchener was born in 1850, the son of an army man. After the death of his mother when he was fourteen, he grew up shy and inward. At the behest of his father, he went to a military academy—not the glamorous training grounds of future military heroes at Sandhurst, however, but the Royal Military Academy at Woolwich, where he found the study of military engineering suited his precise mind. After graduation, he joined the Royal Engineer Corps and served in the Middle East, where he learned Arabic and made a name for himself as a bright, ambitious young officer.

Eventually, he transferred to Egypt, served on the expedition that sought unsuccessfully to relieve Charles Gordon at Khartoum, fought in numerous battles against the Mahdist forces (in one, a glancing dervish bullet left a scar across his face, adding to his formidable appearance) and was rewarded, at the age of forty-two, by being named *Sirdar* (Commander) of the Egyptian army in 1892. He was still in this position when Lord Salisbury ordered the destruction of Mahdist forces in Sudan in 1896.

The key to this operation was taking the Mahdist capital of Omdurman, on the west bank of the Nile River, across from Khartoum, for whoever controlled Omdurman controlled the river and the entire Nile Valley. But how to get there from Egypt? One reason for the failure of Charles Gordon's expedition was that he and his men had had to drag boats south down the Nile, which was marked at stages by treacherous rapids and waterfalls.

Essential supplies and men were lost in this arduous process. But the only alternative for Gordon would have been to march his men straight across the Nubian Desert, an arid sandstone plateau that covers 400,000 square kilometres (155,000 square miles), receives virtually no rainfall, has almost no oases, and where the average daily temperature in June (the hottest month) is 43 degrees Celsius (109 degrees Fahrenheit).

Kitchener, with his passionless but exacting engineer's eye, saw this as a fascinating challenge. After carefully studying maps of the region, he decided that if he could at least take his army down the Nile to the point where the cataracts made it virtually impossible to continue, he could then strike off across the Nubian Desert and reach Atbara, 600 kilometres (375 miles) away, where the Nile became navigable again. Not that Kitchener's army would walk through the blazing landscape of this arid land. They would ride.

## The Sudan Military Railway

Kitchener had decided that he would build a railway across the desert. Most commanders would not even have thought of attempting this feat, but

Kitchener considered it the obvious thing to do. And he took his time about it. He first built up his Anglo–Egyptian force until it was a formidable one. Although still outnumbered by the roughly 50,000 dervishes the Khalifah could field, Kitchener's army eventually consisted of about 8200 British regulars and 17,000 Egyptian and Sudanese soldiers.

Knowing that the railway would only take him to Atbara—still over 300 kilometres (185 miles) from Omdurman—Kitchener also ordered armed river steamers, made in London in prefabricated sections, to be carted along on the railway once it was built, and then assembled at Atbara. These gunboats carried extraordinary firepower—thirty-six artillery pieces and twenty-four Maxim guns—the like of which no Mahdist army had ever seen.

The building of the railway began on 1 January 1897, using forced labour provided by Egyptian soldiers and prisoners. The English journalist G.W. Steevens surveyed the construction at first hand, noting that Kitchener's 'machine-like precision' gave him the confidence to be daring: 'He actually launched his rails ... into the desert while the other end of the line [Atbara] was still held by the enemy'. However, as progress on the tracks went forwards, the men suffered severely from thirst, despite some water being discovered in deep wells bored in the ground.

It was slow going; the railway had to carry not only supplies for those thousands engaged in building it, but also the raw materials for the tracks, since there was no wood for ties, let alone metal for rails, where the railway was going, just, according to Steevens: 'yellow sand to the right and left … stretching away endlessly'. Day after day, the railway moved forwards. The Khalifah heard of its progress, but apparently did not quite believe that the British could pull this off—there had been other, abortive attempts at railways across the Sudan. Steevens saw old engines and rusty parts strewn in the yellow sand, reminders of what could happen to this attempt.

After about a year, by the beginning of January 1898, the railway was 240 kilometres (150 miles) from Atbara. The Khalifah had finally begun to believe the stories that Kitchener was coming across the Nubian Desert, and started to organise against him. On 8 April, 16,000 dervishes attacked a British force that had arrived to secure Atbara in advance of the railway. After a fight, the Mahdist army was bloodily repulsed, and thereafter the Khalifah decided to risk everything on a massive pitched battle when the British arrived outside his capital of Omdurman.

On 14 July 1898, the Sudan Military Railway finally reached Atbara. This extraordinary feat of engineering meant that British troops and supplies that might previously have taken at least four months to make it south from Cairo could now arrive in eleven days. Winston Churchill, travelling with the expedition as a war correspondent, later declared that 'the Khalifah was conquered on the railway'.

### Firepower Wins the Day

After the British force arrived at Atbara, Kitchener assembled his formidable flotilla of gunboats. While it sailed down the Nile, the bulk of the Anglo–Egyptian army marched, by foot and camel, to Omdurman, and set up an encampment on the west bank of the Nile, north of the capital, in early September. There, Kitchener constructed a typically methodical defence: a semicircular *zeriba*—a wall made of mimosa thornbushes—1.5 kilometres (1 mile) long and anchored against the river, where his patrolling gunboats made sure that no one tried to attack from the east bank. His troops stood guard behind the *zeriba* in a classic British formation: two lines of soldiers, the front line kneeling, the back line standing directly behind. Inside the *zeriba* were field pieces and Maxim machine guns (in addition to the ones on the gunboats). The infantry were armed with the Lee-Medford MK II rifle, the finest infantry weapon in the world at the time, a repeating rifle that a trained soldier could fire fifteen times a minute.

The Khalifah had certain choices: instead of fighting the British here, he could retreat, drawing them into a war of attrition in the desert; or he could attack them at night, when their advantage in firepower would be diminished. But, instead, he chose a glorious but foolhardy tactic: a massed attack in broad daylight.

At dawn on 8 September, holding some of his forces in reserve, the Mahdist leader sent about 12,000 screaming dervishes against the British lines. It was an extraordinary sight. Most of the dervishes were infantry, dressed in jihadist white, carrying swords, spears and, in many cases, rifles. Leading them were their emirs, on black Arabian stallions, carrying gigantic banners.

British artillery opened up when the Mahdist warriors were just over 2 kilometres (1¼ miles) away, found the range quite easily and began blowing them to bits—a watching Winston Churchill saw shells obliterating five Sudanese warriors with every burst. Then the Maxim guns, firing at 500 bullets per minute, tore huge holes in the Mahdist lines. Still the enemy kept coming. When the dervishes were a kilometre (half a mile) or so distant, the Anglo–Egyptian infantry opened up with their rifles. Now, with all the modern weapons available to them, the British wreaked a horrific toll. Not one dervish made it to within 300 metres (980 feet) of the *zeriba*. Finally, about two hours later, Kitchener, in typical fashion, ordered the firing to stop: 'Cease fire, please. Cease fire! Cease fire! What a dreadful waste of ammunition!'

### 'The Most Signal Triumph'

The battle was not yet over. Kitchener, seeking to avoid street-fighting in Omdurman, moved his forces out to chase the retreating dervishes, where they were ambushed by the rest of the Khalifah's infantry. The Twenty-first Lancers, young Lieutenant Winston Churchill's regiment, was nearly annihilated because it attacked prematurely, launching a dramatic cavalry charge. But here, too, superior firepower won the day. In the end, the British took Omdurman, driving the Khalifah out (he was chased down the following year and killed), and their takeover of the Nile Valley was complete. The Mahdists lost 10,000 dead, 16,000 wounded, 5000 captured—a horrific 65 per cent casualty rate; the Anglo–Egyptian army suffered 48 men killed and 382 wounded.

The victory at Omdurman was, according to Winston Churchill, 'the most signal triumph ever gained by the arms of science over barbarians'. He was referring not only to modern firepower tearing apart men charging with spears and swords, but also to Kitchener's amazing feat of building a railway across a trackless desert and transporting an army across it. Even today, Kitchener's creation of the Sudan Military Railway ranks as a remarkable achievement in engineering, as well as an ingenious military strategy marked by vision and daring.

# CHAPTER TWELVE

# Admiral Togo's U-Turn
## The Battle of Tsushima, 1905

Until the advent of the aircraft carrier during the Second World War, twentieth-century naval battles were dominated by clashes between fleets of massive steel battleships, characterised by shrieking shells, huge geysers of water, flaming hulls and stricken ships slowly keeling over and sliding beneath the waves. Though iron battleships appeared as early as the mid nineteenth century and steel was used from the 1870s onwards, the first major clash of these behemoth vessels did not take place until 1905, in the chilly waters of the Tsushima Straits off Korea, when the Japanese destroyed Russia's mighty Baltic Fleet with a perfect storm of 2000 high-explosive shells a minute, fired from unheard-of distances.

As well as being the first great naval engagement of the twentieth century, the Battle of Tsushima had major and lasting implications. It helped Japan become a world power, a country the West was forced to deal with on equal terms. It began a race among the world's great navies to build bigger, more powerful battleships, resulting in the mighty dreadnoughts that would clash in the First World War. And it dealt yet another blow to the prestige of the faltering Russian Romanoff dynasty, which would collapse just over a decade later.

But one of the most fascinating things about the battle was the strategy employed by the Japanese commander, a British-educated son of a samurai, Admiral Heihachiro Togo. He took his entire fleet and made a U-turn in front of the Russian fleet. If you or I do a U-turn in traffic, we run the risk of being hit broadside by an oncoming car. That was the risk Admiral Togo took, except on a much larger scale, for the vulnerable flanks of his ships might easily have been devastated by hundreds of 12-inch (30-centimetre) shells. That he triumphed is one of the great stories in the history of naval combat.

### A Naval Education

The Battle of Tsushima has been declared, by contemporary historian Edmund Morris, 'the greatest naval engagement since Trafalgar'. That's fitting, since Togo, the chief architect of this victory, was a great admirer of Admiral Lord Nelson, commander of the British fleet in that 1805 battle. Togo was born in 1848 in southern Japan, at a time when the country was still isolated from the West—as it had been for 200 years—and ruled by a shogun. Togo's father was a *daimyo*, a samurai warrior with the status of a feudal lord.

During his early life, Togo saw Japan, and ways of making war, change with dramatic speed. The US Commodore Matthew Perry visited Japan in 1853; his fleet included two steamships that astonished the cloistered country, whose only vessels were wind-driven. Trade with the West began after this, as did conflict. When samurai warriors murdered a British merchant who had slighted a Japanese lord, the British Royal Navy paid a visit to the port of Kagoshima, near Togo's home village, and demanded that the killers be executed. The Japanese refused and the fifteen-year-old Togo then watched as the British destroyed most of the town in six hours of concentrated gunnery. It was a lesson not lost on him, or on Japan. Soon after, a civil war began, in which the shogun was deposed by forces loyal to the Emperor Meiji—the event that initiated the imperial government of modern Japan. The opposing forces developed small fleets of paddle-wheel steamships, and Togo fought as a gunner and third mate in these battles, gaining valuable experience.

In 1871, the Japanese government sent the young officer, along with a group of his peers, to study naval tactics in Great Britain. Despite the fact that British cadets taunted him as 'Johnny Chinaman' (they were unable to tell one Asian from another), he excelled and graduated second in his class from the Thames Nautical Training College, where he trained and lived aboard a Royal Navy vessel. He also gained experiences few other Japanese naval officers at the time were allowed— in 1875, for example, he circumnavigated the globe as an able seaman.

It was in Britain, too, that Togo first learned about Horatio Nelson and his famous and un- orthodox victory at the Battle of Trafalgar, where, rather than adhering to the convention of drawing his ships up parallel to the enemy, Nelson drove them straight at the opposing fleet. The success of the tactic relied entirely on speed—something Togo would always remember.

## Build-up to War

In the twenty-five years between 1880 and the Battle of Tsushima, Japan's navy grew to become one of the most powerful in the world. There was plenty of opportunity for the expanding Japanese navy—and Togo—to practise tactics. During the Sino–Japanese War in 1894, Togo saw combat with the Japanese fleet that destroyed a larger Chinese armada in the Yellow Sea. Suing for peace, China was forced to cede Japan a good deal of territory, including Formosa (present-day Taiwan), and to give up its claim to Korea. Then the Russians stepped in to grab territory, including large amounts of land in Manchuria and Korea. It was only a matter of time before the two burgeoning powers would clash.

By 1904, when Togo was named commander in chief of the Combined Fleet of Imperial Japan, the Japanese navy had six battleships (purchased from Great Britain), twenty-four cruisers, twenty destroyers and fifty-eight torpedo boats, and was ready to do battle. At the beginning of that year, a series of confrontations escalated tensions between Russia and Japan, and the two countries broke off diplomatic relations on 6 February. Two days later (and two days before war was officially declared), obviously prepared for this, Togo launched a surprise attack against the Russian Pacific Fleet, at harbour in Port Arthur, Manchuria. Ten destroyers attacked and damaged two Russian battleships and a cruiser—not as critical a blow as the Japanese were to strike in another surprise attack, at Pearl Harbor, thirty-seven years later, but enough to put the Russians on notice that this upstart new power was not to be trifled with.

In August of that year, the Pacific Fleet, bottled up in Port Arthur by Togo's ships, attempted to make a break for the port of Vladivostok, 2500 kilometres (1500 miles) north, but Togo intercepted it and, in the Battle of the Yellow Sea, fighting with a squadron of only four hastily assembled battleships, forced the Russians to return to Port Arthur.

Despite these preliminary Japanese naval victories, however, the land war in Manchuria bogged down in a bloody and seemingly interminable First World War–like conflict of attrition, with the Japanese unable to destroy the Russian army. All of this meant that the impending confrontation between the rest of the powerful Russian fleet and the Japanese under Admiral Togo would be crucial to the outcome of the war.

## Facing Off

Even after the destruction of its Pacific Fleet, the Russians remained a formidable sea power. The Russian fleet stationed in the Baltic, then under the command of Admiral Zinovy Petrovich Rozhestvensky, was renamed the Second Pacific Fleet and ordered to sail to Port Arthur to confront the Japanese navy. Beginning on 15 October 1904, the Second Pacific Fleet made a truly incredible 30,000-kilometre (19,000-mile) journey: via the North Sea and English Channel, past Spain and Portugal, all the way down the west coast of Africa, around the Cape of Good Hope, past Madagascar, across the Indian Ocean and into the Pacific. It was an extraordinary but exhausting accomplishment. The tired sailors' morale wasn't helped any when the Russians learned that Port Arthur had fallen to Japanese infantry and that the remains of the Russian fleet there had been destroyed by land-based Japanese artillery.

Nevertheless, as it steamed into the Pacific, Rozhestvensky's proud yellow-and-black-painted armada was a redoubtable sight. The Second Pacific Fleet had fourteen large warships (eleven battle-ships and three cruisers), as well as destroyers and torpedo boats, compared to Japan's twelve warships (four battleships, eight cruisers). But the more significant difference was qualitative. Togo had placed a premium on speed for his battleships and they could outrun most of the Russian ships by at least 3 or 4 knots. In addition, the Japanese had developed a new type of shell containing a material they called *shimose* (essentially, the highly inflammatory and sensitive explosive substance called melinite). These had four times the explosive force of Russian shells and, while not armour-piercing, released clouds of a poisonous gas containing picric acid on contact. The Japanese were also better gunners, trained incessantly to the point where they could hit distant targets accurately while firing at twice the rate of the Russians.

Knowing that the fleet at Port Arthur was destroyed, Admiral Rozhestvensky's goal was to link up with the remaining Russian fleet in Vladivostok, now the only port open to him. In order to do this, he could travel east of the Japanese islands, or he could take a much more direct passage through the Tsushima Strait, which lay between the southeastern corner of the Korean Peninsula and the island of Tsushima. Given his lack of fuel, the Tshushima

Strait was the better option, perhaps his only one. The problem was, the Japanese had already figured he would take this approach, and Togo's fleet was patrolling the waterway in force.

Late on the night of 26 May 1905, the Russian ships entered the strait, travelling at 9 knots, under blackout conditions. They managed to get past the first line of Japanese cruisers and destroyers, but then two Russian hospital ships, lagging several kilometres behind and fully lit up (according to international rules), were spotted by a Japanese cruiser. The captain immediately sent word to Admiral Togo at his base on the southern coast of Korea, opposite Tsushima Island: 'Enemy's smoke in sight'. The main Japanese fleet at once set out to intercept the Russians.

Leading the Japanese fleet around to the north of Tsushima Island to meet the Russians, who were approaching from the south, Togo, in his battleship *Mikasa*, spotted the Russian fleet about 13 kilometres (8 miles) away. It was 1.45 pm. The big Russian battleships led the way, divided into two columns, moving at about 10 knots. Admiral Togo sent out a signal: 'The fate of the empire depends upon this event. Let every man do his utmost'.

## Daring to Cross the 'T'

Togo was now heading right at the enemy; if he kept on in the direction he was going, he ran the real risk of placing his line of ships right between the double line of Russian vessels—and being blasted out of the water from salvoes on each side. Yet if he moved his warships to the east, the Russians could easily slide right by him and head north, aiming for sanctuary in Vladivostok. And this Togo would not allow.

Most commanders in this situation would have turned their ships in place so that Japanese ships could head north in a battle line parallel to that of the Russians. But in doing so, the normal Japanese battle line would have been reversed, and Togo's weakest ships, his cruisers, put under the withering fire of the powerful Russian battleships at the head of the enemy line of battle.

Togo assessed this in just a few minutes, and then made a daring and now famous strategic move. To the astonishment of the watching Russians, he first ordered his ships, beginning with the *Mikasa*, to turn across the line of the advancing Russian fleet. This manoeuvre was known as 'crossing the T', the approaching Russians forming the stem of the 'T' and the Japanese, with their movement, creating the horizontal line at the top. It was a highly risky manoeuvre, for it allowed the Russians a perfect opportunity to pour fire into the flanks of the turning ships, while the Japanese had only the Russian bows to aim at, a much smaller target.

The Russians on the lead ships watched with amazement. Commander Vladimir Semenoff later wrote, 'I looked and looked and, not believing my eyes, could not put down my glasses'. The Russians hastened to take advantage of this apparent gaffe on the part of Togo, and began firing from a range of 6 kilometres (4 miles), but, as Semenoff recorded, the marksmanship either went awry or shells burst without effect (many of the Russian shells turned out to be duds). Meanwhile, the Japanese moved so quickly that, before the Russians knew it, the enemy ships were well off their port bows. Once there, and with the open-mouthed Russian sailors looking on, the entire Japanese battle line made a U-turn and swiftly aligned itself parallel to the Russian fleet. Semenoff wrote: 'The enemy had finished turning. The twelve [Japanese] ships were in perfect order at close intervals, steaming parallel to us'. The Russian ships, poorly handled by their inexperienced crews, bunched up in confusion. At 2.15 pm, Togo ordered the Japanese to open fire at a distance of more than 6 kilometres (4 miles). This was an extremely long distance for accurate fire at this time, as the Russians had shown, but Togo knew that he could rely on his well-trained gunners, and that this, indeed, was his trump card. Having outmanoeuvred the Russians, he knew he could pick them apart at long range.

The accuracy of the Japanese gunners was astounding. The *shimose* shells exploded ferociously, tearing through the Russian ships and killing and maiming the Russian sailors. The first Russian ship to sink was the *Oslyabya*, followed by Admiral Rozhestvensky's flagship, the *Suvorov* (Rozhestvensky transferred to another ship), followed by the battleships *Alexander III* and *Borodino*. By about seven o'clock that evening, the Russian fleet had been destroyed. After mopping up operations on 28 May, which included capturing a severely wounded Rozhestvensky, the Japanese could claim an extraordinary victory. Out of forty-two Russians ships, thirty-one had been captured or sunk, including every battleship. The Russians lost 4830 dead and 5917 captured; the Japanese losses were 3 torpedo boats and 116 dead.

## A New Naval Era

The defeat at Tsushima forced the Russians to sue for peace, resulting in significant territorial gains for Japan—the Treaty of Portsmouth, which ended the war and was signed in September 1905, essentially gave Japan control of Korea and much of Manchuria. This, plus the immense prestige given by the victory, made Japan the pre-eminent power in Asia, and set the stage for its territorial expansion in the late 1930s. Admiral Togo's victory also marked the beginning of a new naval era dominated by massive steel battleships and their big 12-inch (30-centimetre) guns, which could be fired at much greater ranges than any previous guns and could, on their own, utterly annihilate lesser ships. And, finally, it marked Togo out as a brilliant and innovative strategist, on a par with his great hero, Admiral Lord Nelson.

# CHAPTER THIRTEEN

# King Albert Risks All
## The flooding of Flanders, 1914

If you look at a map of Western Europe, you can see the problem: Belgium is located between France, Germany and Britain, so that when these countries decide to wage war, 'poor little Belgium' (as it was dubbed during the First World War) gets caught in the middle. In the middle of the middle, as it were, are the Belgian plains of Flanders, which extend from northern France to northern Belgium along the North Sea coast. It is a low-lying land, divided north to south by the Yser (IJzer) River, crisscrossed with canals and prone to flooding—Flanders, indeed, means 'flooded land' in Flemish.

This region, particularly the area between the Yser River and the North Sea, was a pretty, pastoral, contented sort of place before October of 1914. It was a country of rich pastures, picturesque villages, ancient battle towers, belfried churches and low, white farmhouses capped with red-tiled roofs. Much of the land was polders—tracts of land that had been reclaimed from the sea. Along the coast were fashionable resorts such as La Panne and St-Idesbald, where the ruling French-speaking elite of the country went to vacation; however, inland, Flemish peasants continued to till the soil as they had done for generations.

Just four years later, Flanders would be a war-torn wreck, what the US historian Winston Groom has called 'a gigantic corpse factory', a place where hundreds of thousands of British, French, German, Belgian and American soldiers had given their lives—so many that their blood soaked deep into the rich soil. The carnage came to be symbolised by the red poppies that grew prolifically in this bloodstained earth, as described in Canadian writer John McCrae's famous poem 'In Flanders Fields':

> *In Flanders fields, the poppies blow*
> *Between the crosses, row on row …*

And had it not been for the Belgian king, Albert I, who summoned the North Sea in to inundate his rich land, the slaughter would have been even worse.

## The Shadows of War

The First World War was the almost inevitable result of a relentless military build-up that began at the end of the Franco–Prussian War of 1870–71. Germany's victory in this war encouraged it to expand its army and navy in the hope of becoming a major world power, and made a bitter enemy of its western neighbour, France.

Coming to power in 1889, Kaiser Wilhelm II, the young, militaristic German ruler, feared that a hostile France might ally itself with Russia to the east and hem Germany in. He also realised that Britain, too, saw Germany as a threat, particularly to its traditional naval dominance, despite the strong ties between the countries' two royal families— Kaiser Wilhelm was a grandson of Queen Victoria and was therefore first cousin of the future British king, George V.

With tensions soaring, all European countries began to arm themselves, and Germany continued to lead the way. The effect of its bellicose stance was to reinforce alliances between France, Britain and Russia aimed at containing it. Regarding this containment as a suffocating encirclement, Germany developed detailed plans for an attack on France and Russia. The precarious situation in the Balkans, where Russia vied with Germany's traditional ally Austria for control of Serbia, soon provided a justification for war.

After a Serbian anarchist assassinated Archduke Franz Ferdinand, the heir to the Austro–Hungarian Hapsburg throne, in Sarajevo on 28 June 1914, Austria invaded Serbia, with Germany's support. Russia mobilised against Austria and Germany, leading Germany to declare war on Russia. With France obliged by treaty to support Russia, the two bitter enemies of the Franco–Prussian War lined up against each other again.

Germany's war plan was known as the Schlieffen Plan, after its creator, Count Alfred von Schlieffen, German Chief of Staff from 1891 to 1905. Perfected by the time of his retirement in 1905, it called for a blocking force to hold the heavily fortified French border while a much larger force marched through neutral Luxembourg and Belgium to the North Sea coast, then swung south around Paris. Inspired by Hannibal's success at Cannae (see p. 23), Schlieffen saw the final outcome as a huge encirclement of the French army, which would be attacked on France's eastern border from front and rear, and destroyed.

When the French were safely pacified, the Germans would turn their attention to their enemies in the east: the Russians.

Speed was of the essence. For his plan to work, Schlieffen calculated that the conquest of France had to be completed in six weeks. Belgium was the only major obstacle, and he foresaw few problems there: it was a small, relatively weak nation, and its defences would be easily overcome—if it even attempted to defend itself at all.

### 'A Nation, Not a Highway'

Belgium had been created in the 1830s from a conglomeration of Flemish states, mainly at the behest of Great Britain. The formation of the new nation was a victory for Britain and its Secretary of State, Lord Palmerston, because it kept France from annexing the country, but this victory came at a price: by treaty, Britain promised to come to the aid of Belgium if ever the country were invaded.

King Albert I was the third king of the Belgians. He came to the throne young, in 1909, and was still just thirty-nine years old when the First World War broke out in 1914. He was a handsome, dark-haired young man, whose informal mode of dress and comportment brought him into the twentieth century ahead of most royalty of the time. Albert was quite religious, and known for being taciturn, but he was not someone who readily gave in to bullying. When Germany's Kaiser Wilhelm (who was, in fact, a distant royal relative) tried to force Albert to allow German troops to move through Belgium on the eve of the First World War, Albert famously replied: 'I rule a nation, not a highway'.

Unfortunately, Belgium was a neutral country and had not participated in the arms build-up of Germany, Britain, France and Russia. Belgian soldiers, while brave, were severely outnumbered and ill-prepared, compared to the Germans. Many units dressed like nineteenth-century grenadiers. They had few machine guns and those they did have were pulled by teams of dogs.

### The Schlieffen Plan Stalls

German Chief of Staff Field Marshal Helmuth von Moltke commanded seven armies totalling about 1.5 million men. As per the Schlieffen Plan, two of these armies were arrayed in a line from the city of Metz all the way to Switzerland, as a blocking force should the French counterattack. The remainder moved northwards. On 4 August 1914, the German First and Second Armies, totalling approximately 600,000 men, crossed the Meuse River and moved against the Belgian fortress of Liège. That same day, Britain, honouring its obligations to Belgium, declared war on Germany.

The Belgians put up an unexpectedly strong resistance, using machine guns and artillery to kill thousands of Germans making frontal attacks (the first of the great slaughters of the Great War) until Major General Erich Ludendorff took one brigade and managed to capture Liège. The two German armies then advanced, pushing the Belgian field army back further and further. Brussels was abandoned and the Germans entered the city in triumph on 20 August, while Belgian forces under King Albert retreated towards Antwerp.

What should have been the beginning of a magnificent German victory, however, was marred by a series of outrages perpetrated on the Belgians, including at least three large-scale massacres of hundreds of defenceless civilians, among them many women and children. Moreover, the unexpected resistance of the Belgians had slowed the German advance considerably.

Large numbers of refugees fled before the German armies. Now and again, the Belgians would turn and fight a delaying action in the blazing hot August weather, with rifles and machine guns chattering. King Albert rallied his troops enough to give the French army time to attack from the south, while the British Expeditionary Force (BEF) crossed the English Channel, landed at Le Havre and immediately threw itself into the fray. But the better prepared Germans began to push the French and British south, and the Belgians were forced to retreat north and west, towards the sea.

By the end of August, five German armies—a million men—were stretched from Liège to the outskirts of Paris (German officers could see the Eiffel Tower through binoculars). But then Moltke, seeking to strengthen his right wing, which was fighting furthest to the north, in Belgium, withdrew forces from the area around Paris, and the French counterattacked.

In the Battle of the Marne, Moltke was defeated, suffered a nervous collapse and was replaced. It was now mid September and the Schlieffen Plan, which was supposed to have taken six weeks to complete, was hopelessly stalled. Moreover, both the Germans and the Allies realised that their northern flanks were not anchored—that they had not reached the North Sea, in other words, and were thus unprotected.

## A Desperate Race

There now began what became known as the Race to the Sea. In an amazing series of manoeuvres, the armies of the British and French and those of the Germans began to leapfrog each other as they moved back north. They dug in as they went, seeking to place themselves one step ahead of the enemy. The Germans wanted to turn the Allied flank and reach the Channel ports; the Allies wanted to keep the Germans from doing that and, if possible, turn their flanks. Ten separate battles occurred as the antagonists clashed bitterly.

The manoeuvres took the warring foes straight back to Belgium, where King Albert had emplaced his army around Antwerp and was strongly resisting the German advance. Everyone knew the fighting would not stop until one of the armies breached the other's flank—or they reached the North Sea. If no flank was turned, the entire front would more than likely be gripped in a stalemate.

German forces began targeting Antwerp with their howitzers on 27 September, launching an awesome display of firepower. The poet Rupert Brooke, a lieutenant with the BEF, watched the destruction and called it 'one of the greatest crimes of history'. Thousands of civilians and soldiers were slaughtered until King Albert abandoned the city on 6 October and evacuated west to the sea with his five weary Belgian divisions.

By then, the forces of all of the antagonists were concentrated in Flanders—formerly lovely, quiet, pastoral Flanders—a total, historians later estimated, of 300,000 Allied soldiers and 500,000 Germans, facing each other on a battlefield about 65 kilometres (40 miles) long. Though the soldiers dug trenches, they were not the elaborate variety seen later in the war; these were simply connected foxholes, or shallow ditches. Sometimes the men on both sides simply sheltered behind trees and in ruined houses, since the water tables in Flanders (water underlay everything, up to a metre [3 feet] beneath the soil) made serious digging difficult.

German and Allied forces were concentrated most strongly around the central Flanders town of Ypres, a city renowned for its cloth merchants.

On 20 October, the first Battle of Ypres took place
(there would be two more during the war, which
would claim in total over a million lives) as the
British and French sought to pulverise the German
right flank and drive it away from the North Sea. In a
bloody coincidence, the Germans opened their own
attack at the same time to try to break through to the
Channel. Wave after wave of German troops met the
Allies in desperate fighting along the Yser River.

Young German soldiers died by the thousands
at the hands of the French, British and Belgians,
but their overwhelming superiority in numbers
began to tell. By 21 October, the Allied forces were
being pushed back everywhere across the Flanders
plains. Beleaguered BEF forces and Belgian soldiers held a line from Ypres to the village of
Diksmuide, but between Diksmuide and the coastal
town of Nieuwpoort was a wide gap through which
the rallying German forces would almost certainly
attack, turning the Allied flank.

### An Agonising Decision

King Albert, who had retreated to a Belgian seaside
village, knew that if something wasn't done,
Belgium was lost and the Allied cause in peril.

Along the coast, the Germans were being held back only by the fierce fire of British battleships in the North Sea. A small force of Belgian soldiers and Flemish sailors held Diksmuide, but then, on 21 October, the Germans opened up their powerful guns and reduced that village to rubble. The way to Nieuwpoort was opening up, along with the all-important railway line that ran between Diksmuide and the seaport.

There is some question as to whose idea it was to open the sluices and floodgates to inundate the land and thereby create a water barrier to the German advance. Some historians attribute the plan to a Belgian general, others to a group of Flemish civilians. But once it was brought to King Albert, he did not hesitate. Even though he knew that flooding the land would cause severe hardship for his people in years to come, on 27 October he ordered that the floodgates be opened, that the sea be let in.

The people of Flanders had spent much of their history keeping the sea out, and now they were allowing the water to inundate their land, so this was no small thing. Many, if not most, of the Belgian civilians in the areas to be affected had already fled the conflict, but those who had not yet evacuated were now forced to leave their homes, in the certain knowledge that their farms and businesses would be severely affected by the rising water (and in fact it would not be until 1920 that the land would grow crops again). Yet the Belgian people knew they had no choice, and most supported their king's decision: without this desperate gambit, they would be overwhelmed by the German forces, whose reputation for cruelty now preceded them.

The Belgian army, with the assistance of the civilian engineers in charge of the sluices and floodgates, went into action. The night of 29 October saw a full moon, which created the right tidal conditions—as high a tide as possible was needed, in order to ensure that the waters rushed in with maximum effect.

The main sluices of the canal system were at Nieuwpoort, and these were exploded with enormous quantities of dynamite. Other, smaller sluices had to be held open manually in order to permit enough water to flow in. In the meantime, Allied troops took up high positions atop canal walls and riverbanks.

## A Signal Service to the Cause

The first sign the Germans had of the Belgian operation was when water began to flow into their trenches. Nevertheless, even as the waters were rising, they made a last, desperate attack, sloshing through ankle-deep sheets of water. But they were beaten back by the much better positioned and better prepared Allies.

Within about a week, the North Sea floodwaters had risen to cover the land from Nieuwpoort to Diksmuide, a distance of 16 kilometres (10 miles). The water was over 3 kilometres (2 miles) wide and more than a metre (3 feet) deep. Even if the Germans had been able to find sufficient shallow-draft boats to transport thousands upon thousands of troops, they would have become sitting ducks for Allied artillery and machine-gun fire.

Belgium—and the entire Allied line—was now safe from being outflanked. Indeed, the Germans were never able to overcome this artificial water barrier for the duration of the war. Effectively stalemated, they were forced to engage in the long, attritional campaign that came to characterise the First World War. The Belgians—outnumbered and outgunned—had done extraordinarily well. As one

British diplomat put it at the time: 'In this fine defence, which did honour to all the troops and commanders engaged in it, the Belgians performed a signal service to the Allied cause'.

# CHAPTER FOURTEEN

## Ghostly Retreat
### The Japanese withdrawal from Kiska, 1943

During the Pacific Island fighting of the Second World War, the Japanese gained a well-deserved reputation for never retreating without a fight to the death. Even when completely surrounded on some desperate battle-torn atoll, with no chance whatsoever of finding their way out, Japanese troops routinely killed themselves before withdrawing or giving up. This is why it is all the more surprising to learn that in 1943 the Japanese initiated one of the most brilliant tactical withdrawals of the entire war: 6000 soldiers of the Japanese Imperial Army stole away so quietly from the island of Kiska, in the Aleutian chain off Alaska, that American forces subsequently bombed the uninhabited island for two whole weeks, mounted a full-scale invasion with 35,000 troops and fought a pitched battle—against each other—that resulted in hundreds of casualties.

As with many successful unconventional tactical manoeuvres, the Japanese took their enemy's expectations and turned them on their head. And, since the episode occurred in the Aleutians, they also had a little help from the weather.

## No Place to Fight a War

Even for those who love wilderness, salt air and mountains, the Aleutian archipelago can seem a godforsaken place. The islands stretch in a semi-circle for 1600 kilometres (1000 miles) across the Bering Sea from the southwestern tip of Alaska all the way to within 50 kilometres (30 miles) of Siberia's Kamchatka Peninsula. Closest to Alaska are the bigger islands of Unimak and Unalaska (with its port at Dutch Harbor); furthest into the ocean are the tiny islands of Attu and Kiska.

The Aleutians—the name comes probably from the Aleut Indian word *aliat*, or island—may have formed the land bridge by which some of the earliest peoples occupied North America. The first European to come across the islands was Aleksey Chirikov, a Russian captain temporarily separated from Vitus Bering's 1741 expedition to Alaska. Bering himself landed on several of the islands in the sea that would later bear his name, before finally becoming marooned in the Commander Islands off the Kamchatka Peninsula and dying there.

For the next hundred years or so, the Aleutians were populated mainly by Siberian seal hunters and Aleut natives. Even after the United States bought Alaska from Russia in 1867, they were visited by few people. Hardy travellers who did venture there found rocky and treeless expanses towered over by dead volcanoes (fifty-seven in the archipelago in all) and drenched by almost constant rain—the Aleutians receive the greatest amount of rainfall in the United States, with Unalaska, for example, having 250 days of rain a year. A low-pressure system is almost permanently in place over the islands, covering them with dense fogs that hug ground and ocean. And when it isn't foggy or rainy, the wind howls, hard—160 kilometres per hour (100 miles per hour) is fairly commonplace.

By any standards, the Aleutians are a tough place to fight a war, but by the late 1930s, with both the Japanese and American military sure that conflict was imminent, it looked like they would soon become a battleground. From the Japanese perspective, they were the closest bit of America to Japan. The Japanese had been spying on the Aleutians for years in the 1930s, using 'fishing' fleets that took soundings of harbours and charted shorelines. If they could use the Aleutians as stepping stones to invade and gain a foothold on mainland Alaska, they would only be a three-hour flight from Seattle and its massive Boeing bomber plant. They could also use Alaska as a base from which to strike at Russia, just across the Bering Strait.

Despite being aware of this threat, the US military did little to fortify the Aleutians, though they did have small garrisons on Attu and Kiska, and airstrips and naval facilities on eastern islands including Unimak and Unalaska, which were closer to the mainland and easier to supply. After the attack on Pearl Harbor on 7 December 1941, however, most of America's attention was focused on the South Pacific and East Asia—even more so after the Battle of the Coral Sea in May of 1942, which saw the Americans lose two aircraft carriers to the Japanese Imperial Navy. At this high point in Japanese fortunes, Admiral Isoroku Yamamoto was planning the coup de grace against the American navy, a top-secret plan known as the MI Operation. The Combined Imperial Fleet would sortie to the vicinity of Midway Island in the central Pacific, to destroy the remaining American carriers. At the same time, a large Japanese invasion force would head for the Aleutians, to threaten the United States. When the Americans realised this, they would leave their bases and race for the North Pacific—at which point Yamamoto would intercept them near Midway and destroy them.

## The Tide Turns at Midway

The question for Admiral Chester Nimitz, commander in chief of American naval forces in the Pacific, was, where would it do the most good to place his diminished naval forces. Dividing them would give him almost no chance of defeating Yamamoto at Midway, but leaving the Aleutians undefended would permit a Japanese invasion of Alaska and cut off important American shipping lanes in the Bering Sea.

In the end, Nimitz opted for a compromise that would shape the course of the fifteen-month-long campaign in the Aleutians: he would send a small force there, just large enough to delay the Japanese, while he concentrated most of his navy, including his two remaining aircraft carriers, at Midway.

So began the most momentous few days in the history of the Pacific War. On 4 June, the Americans and Japanese clashed at Midway, in a large-scale naval action that turned out to be a disastrous defeat for Yamamoto—he lost all four of his aircraft carriers along with 300 planes and over 3000 Japanese lives. The day before, the Japanese navy had approached the Aleutian Islands in force, bringing two aircraft carriers, six heavy cruisers, a screen of submarines and destroyers, and troop transports containing 2500 Japanese marines.

The commander of the North Pacific Fleet was Admiral Boshiro Hosogaya. During the preliminary phase of his attack, he sent planes off to bomb Dutch Harbor, the main American base on Unalaska Island, causing considerable damage. But he subsequently received dispatches from Yamamoto describing the disastrous Japanese defeat at Midway; Yamamoto ordered Hosogaya and his carriers to steam south to protect the withdrawal of the battered Japanese fleet.

Then, almost immediately, Yamamoto countermanded these orders; he had realised that even a small success, like the occupation of the Aleutian Islands, was needed now. So he ordered Hosogaya to occupy the islands furthest from the range of the American bombers based in Dutch Harbor and Unimak: Attu and Kiska.

## The Forgotten War

The Japanese marines easily conquered Attu and Kiska—the former had no American forces, the latter only a small group of sailors manning a radio outpost. For the first time, Japanese forces were officially occupying American soil. For the Japanese people—who were not told of the defeat at Midway—this was a momentous victory. For the Americans, it created, coming after more Japanese I-boat submarine attacks on the West Coast, a serious threat to national morale: if the Japanese had been destroyed at Midway, what were they doing in Alaska, and sending submarines to bomb coastal cities with impunity?

There were 2600 Japanese troops on Attu and 6000 on Kiska, but at first the war in the Aleutians was one of savage bomber attacks and fighter encounters, as each side sought to cripple the other, the Japanese forces flying east from Kiska and the Americans flying west from Dutch Harbor. Horseshoe-shaped Kiska Harbor bristled with anti-aircraft emplacements that made bombing runs there as perilous as any that occurred in the European theatre.

But, with the invasion of North Africa then taking place and battles raging in the Solomon Islands, the Aleutian front was quickly forgotten, and both sides suffered privations as a result. Supplies, including winter clothes, had to be scrounged; fishing and hunting were permitted to supplement rations. The Japanese troops were perhaps better prepared, having warmer footwear; some of them even spent their spare time skiing. On Kiska, they lived in a huge underground base, to protect them from bombers; they also built three hospitals, a dental clinic and a telephone switchboard.

Gradually, however, the Americans built up their forces for an invasion of Attu, which took place eleven months after the Japanese occupied the island. On 11 May 1943, US troops landed on the frozen island, expecting a three-day-long battle. It ended up taking three weeks. Japanese resistance was ferocious, finishing with a fierce banzai attack that caught the Americans by surprise. Of the 2600 Japanese, only 28 survived. The Americans suffered about 3800 casualties, including 500 killed.

Proportionate to the forces involved, Attu would end up being America's second most costly battle during the Pacific War in terms of loss of lives, the bloody assault on Iwo Jima being the first.

## Planning the Withdrawal

The Battle of Attu convinced American planners that they had not taken the Japanese forces in the Aleutians seriously enough, so when they planned for the invasion of Kiska, they allotted 30,000 US troops and 5000 Canadian soldiers to the attack—more than twice as many as had landed on Attu—and set the date for mid August.

The only problem was, the Japanese weren't planning on being there. In the summer of 1943, after the invasion of Attu, Aleutian-based bombers began raiding Japanese bases in the Kuril Islands, particularly on the fortress island of Paramushiro (now Russian-controlled Paramushir). The Kurils guarded the northernmost approach to Japan, and the Japanese high command became convinced that forces on Kiska would be better deployed there. But how to get them off Kiska? The Americans were blockading the island and bombing it daily—it would only be a matter of time before they invaded.

The Japanese began sending I-boats to Kiska, and eventually managed to evacuate about 600 soldiers, but this was dangerous: the American fleet located three of the submarines and destroyed them, killing 300 Japanese troops. Time was running out. Finally, Vice Admiral Shiro Kawase, by then in charge of Japan's Northern Pacific forces, concocted a daring plan. Back on Paramushiro, he put together an evacuation force consisting of three cruisers, eleven destroyers and a refuelling tanker. 'Taking advantage of dense fog', he wrote, he would 'evacuate all men [from Kiska] simultaneously'.

Fortunately, by this time in the war, the Japanese had changed their naval communications codes, so that the Americans, who had previously broken the top-secret Japanese ciphers, did not become aware of this plan. The Japanese commander on Kiska, who had been preparing for the death of himself and all his men, was instructed that a rescue fleet would soon be arriving.

## An Invisible Manoeuvre

On 21 July, the Japanese evacuation fleet steamed south, making a wide circle below Kiska to evade US forces and aircraft. Reaching their assigned coordinates 800 kilometres (500 miles) south of Kiska, the ships waited for fog—for only under a thick cloak of cloud could they possibly approach the Aleutians, which swarmed with hostile US shipping preparing to invade the island.

On 26 July, the Japanese finally got the weather they needed. Vice Admiral Kawase and his fleet entered a large fog bank and moved with it to a point 80 kilometres (50 miles) off Kiska. Their luck held and the Americans failed to spot them, though the Japanese lost five of their ships in a multiple-ship collision in the fog, the damaged vessels being forced to limp back home. On the morning of 27 July, the weather worsened. Deciding he did not have enough time to wait for nightfall—the Americans were bombing Kiska furiously—Kawase sent the Japanese fleet steaming into Kiska Harbor.

The 5000 Japanese soldiers on Kiska were ready to leave. They had destroyed gun emplacements, booby-trapped their underground facilities and scrawled obscene messages for the Americans on the walls. Now, in one of the most brilliant manoeuvres of the Second World War, two Japanese cruisers took off about 2400 of the soldiers and six destroyers carried off the rest. By 7.30 pm, the evacuation had been completed—without a single injury. With the fog lifting, the Japanese fleet sailed at full speed out of Kiska. Four days later, Vice Admiral Kawase arrived, undetected by the Americans, in Paramushiro.

For two weeks before the 15 August date set for the invasion of Kiska, the Americans battered the island with enormous barrages of high explosives. They even dropped leaflets calling on the Japanese to surrender—leaflets that fluttered down onto a deserted island. Finally, on the morning of 15 August, thousands of American and Canadian troops stormed ashore in thick fog (with more following the next day). Booby traps exploded and jittery soldiers fired at movements in the fog. Other troops fired back. For days, small firefights occurred all over the island. Although many American commanders suspected from the start that the Japanese had left, others thought they were buried in the underground bunkers and needed to be dug out. In the three days before the Allies realised that no one was at home but themselves, more than 300 Americans and Canadians were wounded by friendly fire. Four Canadians and seventeen American soldiers died.

In a war that was now singularly devoid of victories for the Japanese, the retreat from Kiska was something they could finally point to with satisfaction, since they had tied up thousands of US troops and scores of American ships. For a people renowned for fighting to the death, it was a rare kind of victory.

CHAPTER FIFTEEN

# 'This Most Successful Threat'
## Operation Fortitude, 1944

The martial philosopher Sun Tzu once said, 'All warfare is based on deception'. Nothing could be truer. Little kids playing soldier instinctively learn to sneak up on their 'enemy', to lie motionless and 'play dead', to camouflage their faces, to feint left and go right. Big kids involved in world-spanning wars do the same thing, but on an unimaginably massive scale. Operation Fortitude, the Allied plan to convince the Germans that the 1944 invasion of France would strike anywhere but where it actually did, in Normandy, is perhaps the most extraordinary example of deception in war in history. An entire department of the Supreme Headquarters Allied Expeditionary Force (SHAEF), the innocuously named London Controlling Section, spent the better part of a year convincing the German high command that the D-Day invasion would strike the Pas de Calais region, east of the Seine River, rather than the Cotentin Peninsula and Normandy, to the west. Aiding in this crucial charade were numerous German agents who were actually Allied agents (or simply didn't exist at all) and thousands of Allied troops, as well as dummy ships, tanks and aeroplanes. As a result, an entire German army—the German Fifteenth Army—which could have driven the Normandy invaders back into the sea, was held, frozen in place east of the Seine, and untold thousands of lives were saved.

## Need for a Diversion

At the Casablanca Conference, held in January 1943, British Prime Minister Winston Churchill, American President Franklin Delano Roosevelt and Charles de Gaulle, leader of the Free French forces then fighting the Germans, made aggressive plans for the future of the war in Europe. Sicily would be invaded in June of that year, Italy in September. And by the spring of 1944, there would be a cross-Channel invasion of France.

The problem here was that the German high command (OKW) knew they were coming. The entire coast of 'Fortress Europe' (as Hitler called it)—from Holland all the way down to Spain—had been heavily fortified with mines, beach obstacles and seawalls, pillboxes and artillery emplacements. The Germans had also created mobile reserve forces of tanks and infantry located further back from the beaches at strategic locations. Their job was to respond quickly to the particular point where the invasion would take place.

Any trained military planner on either side, looking at a map of France and England, would pick one obvious point for the invasion: Pas de Calais. Not only was this area the closest to England—on a clear day you could look across the Channel from here to the White Cliffs of Dover—but it contained numerous port cities, whose harbours and facilities would be desperately needed by any invading force. From here, the Allies could move in a direct line towards Paris and, ultimately, Berlin.

Allied planners, however, had other ideas. Their plan, dubbed Operation Overlord and submitted for approval in the summer of 1943, was ingenious and audacious. Instead of taking the shortest route across the English Channel, at the Straits of Dover, SHAEF planners instead recommended an invasion of Normandy, specifically the

Cotentin Peninsula. There were no sizable natural harbours here, but so what? SHAEF intended to build its own, with shiploads of materials and concrete docks floated over from England. It also planned to lay an underwater fuel pipeline across the ocean floor from the Isle of Wight.

These were ingenious ideas, but the only way they would work would be if the Allied forces had the element of surprise. If the Germans suspected for one moment that this was the main invasion force, then the Fifteenth Army panzer divisions further north and east would be quickly shifted to Normandy and the American, Canadian and British forces pounded into the sand of their beachheads, before any harbour could be built or pipeline laid.

### 'A Bodyguard of Lies'

In 1943, Winston Churchill commented, 'In wartime, truth is so precious that she should always be accompanied by a bodyguard of lies'. His comment provided a name, Operation Bodyguard, for the overall Allied plan that was needed, as SHAEF put it, 'to deceive the enemy as to the strength, objective and timing of Overlord'. It was decided that the tactical plan of deception itself would be called Operation Fortitude and it would have three main objectives: to convince the Germans that the main attack would take place in Pas de Calais, around 15 July 1944; to convince the Germans that any Normandy invasion was a diversionary attack, not the real thing—and to keep them thinking this for at least two weeks after the actual attack; and to convince the Germans that another attack might come as far north as Norway.

There would be two Fortitudes, then: Fortitude North would create the impression that a flanking invasion was about to take place in Norway, while Fortitude South would aim to convince the Germans that the main invasion would come across the Straits of Dover.

The assignment to oversee and implement these detailed deceptions—where one wrong note might spell death for soldiers of the invading forces—fell to the London Controlling Section, created for just this task, whose bland, bureaucratic-sounding name belied the top-secret nature of its role. It consisted of a small group of officers led by Colonel John Bevan, but the man now almost universally acknowledged as the prime mover behind Operation Fortitude was the operations manager, lawyer Roger

Hesketh. Hesketh was a member of Britain's upper class whose home, Meols Hall in Lancashire, had been in his family for eight centuries, and who had been educated at Eton and Oxford. He had joined the army at the outbreak of the war and had risen through the ranks of British intelligence.

Hesketh and his colleagues had one significant advantage over the Germans: Ultra. This was the code-name for intelligence obtained by decoding German wireless transmissions, in particular the messages encrypted by a highly complex machine called Enigma. With the help of Polish scientists, the British had been able to reconstruct the German machine and, by studying it, a team led by scientists including Alan Turing had managed to crack its supposedly unbreakable code as early as 1940. As a result, Hesketh and others working on Fortitude were able to tell almost immediately if the ruses they were using were having any effect.

### Fictitious Armies

To help convince the Germans that the attack was going to target Pas de Calais, Fortitude South created the impression of a build-up of troops in the southeast through the construction of physical decoys. Dummy airbases and infantry camps, even fake tanks and landing craft, were built by special British and American camouflage units. From the ground, these sheds, tanks and boats, mainly constructed of wood and canvas, looked decidedly fake. However, from a distance, or from a wandering German reconnaissance plane, they seemed like the real deal. (In aerial photographs taken by the British of dummy landing craft in Dover harbour, the fakes can't be told apart from the real thing.)

One of the major achievements of this strategy was to create the belief in the minds of the German high command—and Adolf Hitler—that the First US Army Group (FUSAG), led by General George S. Patton, was in southeastern England, opposite Calais. Fake FUSAG camps and bases were placed around possible embarkation points on the coast there, and an enormous amount of fake radio traffic regarding its presence was engendered. Furthermore, Patton, who was of course quite real, was often seen visiting these locations.

This notable success aside, however, the physical decoy strategy was found to have limited effect. Ironically, Allied air superiority was so complete over Britain, and German reconnaissance so poor, that the Germans seldom noticed the dummy bases. Something further was needed, and for this, Hesketh relied on spies—German spies.

## Imaginary Spies

In early 1944, the Abwehr, the German intelligence service, had fifty agents operating inside Britain. Unbeknown to them, MI5, the British intelligence service, controlled every single one of them. The prime example of this was the agent code-named Garbo by the Allies and Arabel by the Abwehr. His real name, which he agreed to reveal only in the 1980s, was Juan Pujol.

Pujol was born in Spain in 1912 and took a strong dislike to the Nazis during the Spanish Civil War. MI5 brought Pujol to England, gave him a cover story and a case officer, and, most astonishingly, helped him create a system of twenty-four 'subagents'—all of whom were entirely imaginary.

In the run-up to the D-Day invasion, in the winter and spring of 1944, these imaginary agents were put to good use. The subagent known as Seven, for instance, was an ex-seaman whom Pujol described to his Abwehr handler in Madrid as 'a thoroughly undesirable character' who worked solely for money.

But he lived in southeast England and was able to observe the build-up of forces there, presumably for the invasion of Pas de Calais. There were other such 'agents' stationed, supposedly, throughout the country. As Pujol later stated, if one of these agents reported something the Abwehr knew to be false, Pujol could simply blame the imaginary agent for the mistake and 'liquidate' him.

Hesketh never had agents like Garbo merely feed the Germans false documents or information. It was of the utmost importance, when it came to Fortitude, that the Germans decide for themselves, by piecing together reports from various sources, where the invasion was likely to come from. Thus, although Garbo's subagent Seven might report a build-up of men and materiel in southeastern England, Hesketh knew there really had to be troops there, in case someone, somehow, checked.

## Scheming on Two Fronts

Although Fortitude North was secondary to its southern counterpart, it was also an extraordinary undertaking. A fictitious British 'Fourth Army' was created and 'placed' in Scotland, Ireland and Iceland. Only a few visual dummy props were used, due in part to a lack of resources and the fact that there was little German air reconnaissance in these places. Instead, simulated wireless communications were sent out to make the Germans believe that the Fourth Army was there. This was no easy feat, as such communications were studied very closely by Abwehr operatives experienced in unit-to-unit radio contact, and quite aware that such radio chatter could be manufactured as a ruse.

Adding to the verisimilitude was a move to open diplomatic relations with neutral Sweden, with an eye towards having that country give the Allies the right to land and conduct reconnaissance missions from Swedish territory. Hesketh and the Allies knew full well that Sweden was unlikely to grant them these rights—it would then have to grant Germany the same—but they wanted word of the initiative to reach German ears, so that the OKW might deduce that the Allies were preparing an invasion of Norway.

No one quite knows if the deception of Fortitude North worked as well as the Allies hoped—although for whatever reason, German divisions in Norway were reinforced. All told, some 280,000 German troops were stationed in Norway. Had the Germans divined the real intentions of the Allies, they would almost certainly have rushed some of these troops to the south. Fortitude South, however, was, unmistakably, an immense success. The entire German Fifteenth Army—twenty-two divisions, 100,000 men—would be held in place in Pas de Calais as late as two weeks after the Normandy invasion because, as German dispatches said, 'the main [Allied force] has not yet landed'.

## At Last, a Real Invasion

On 6 June 1944, after all the deception, the real attack began in Normandy. Allied parachutists were dropped behind German lines during the night. At first light, German soldiers manning the pillboxes on the Normandy bluffs saw an astonishing sight: 6500 ships, carrying 150,000 men, supported by 11,000 aircraft. The fighting was fierce—there were 9000 Allied casualties—but by the end of the day the American, British and Canadian forces were moving inland. By summer's end, they were in Paris. The Germans had been taken completely by surprise.

As per the original plan, Fortitude South continued to operate after the landing. On 9 June, Garbo sent a message to his Madrid handler saying that FUSAG was still held in place in southeastern England—meaning that this nonexistent army group was still poised in readiness to attack Pas de Calais. Because of this, Hitler himself issued orders that the Fifteenth not be shifted to aid in the defence of Normandy, much to the despair of Field Marshal Erwin Rommel, who was in charge of the Atlantic defences and knew he needed these men and tanks to beat back the Allied invasion.

Soon after D-Day, General Dwight Eisenhower, Supreme Commander of the Allied forces, wrote:

> *Lack of infantry was the most important cause of the enemy's defeat in Normandy, and his failure to remedy this weakness was due primarily to the success of Allied threats levelled against the Pas de Calais … I cannot overemphasise the decisive value of this most successful threat.*

Astonishingly, the Allies weren't the only ones to congratulate Fortitude operatives. On 29 July 1944, Garbo's German handlers in Madrid advised him in a secret communication that Hitler had awarded him the Iron Cross. Even though the Pas de Calais invasion had not occurred, the Germans believed it was simply because the Normandy invasion had been so successful that FUSAG wasn't needed. And so they rewarded Pujol—who also received an MBE from the grateful British—as the good and faithful servant they assumed him to be.

Now, that's deception!

# INDEX

First published in 2010 by Pier 9, an imprint of Murdoch Books Pty Limited

Murdoch Books Australia
Pier 8/9, 23 Hickson Road
Millers Point NSW 2000
Phone: +61 (0) 2 8220 2000
Fax: +61 (0) 2 8220 2558
www.murdochbooks.com.au

Murdoch Books UK Limited
Erico House, 6th Floor North
93/99 Upper Richmond Road
Putney, London SW15 2TG
Phone: +44 (0) 20 8785 5995
Fax: +44 (0) 20 8785 5985
www.murdochbooks.co.uk

Publisher: Diana Hill
Project Manager: Paul O'Beirne
Editor: Scott Forbes
Design: Jenny Grigg

National Library of Australia Cataloguing-in-Publication Data:

| | |
|---|---|
| Title: | Turning the tide of battle. |
| ISBN: | 9781741967258 (pbk) |
| Series: | Pocket history series. |
| Notes: | Includes index. |
| Subjects: | Strategy. |
| | Tactics. |
| | Military art and science. |
| | Special operations (Military science) |
| Dewey Number: | 355.4 |

A catalogue record for this book is available from the British Library.

Printed on FSC-accredited paper. Printed in China.